I0752915

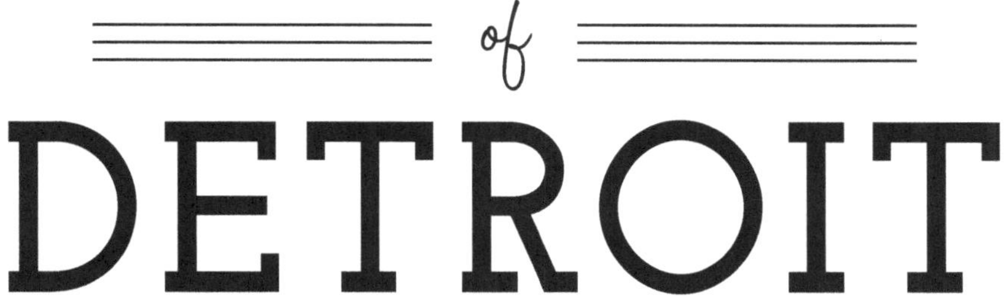
LOST RESTAURANTS
of
DETROIT

LOST RESTAURANTS *of* DETROIT

PAUL VACHON

Published by American Palate
A Division of The History Press
Charleston, SC
www.historypress.net

Copyright © 2016 by Paul Vachon
All rights reserved

Back cover, center: Courtesy of Buddy's Pizza.

First published 2016

Manufactured in the United States

ISBN 978.1.46713.559.7

Library of Congress Control Number: 2016943912

Notice: The information in this book is true and complete to the best of our knowledge. It is offered without guarantee on the part of the author or The History Press. The author and The History Press disclaim all liability in connection with the use of this book.

All rights reserved. No part of this book may be reproduced or transmitted in any form whatsoever without prior written permission from the publisher except in the case of brief quotations embodied in critical articles and reviews.

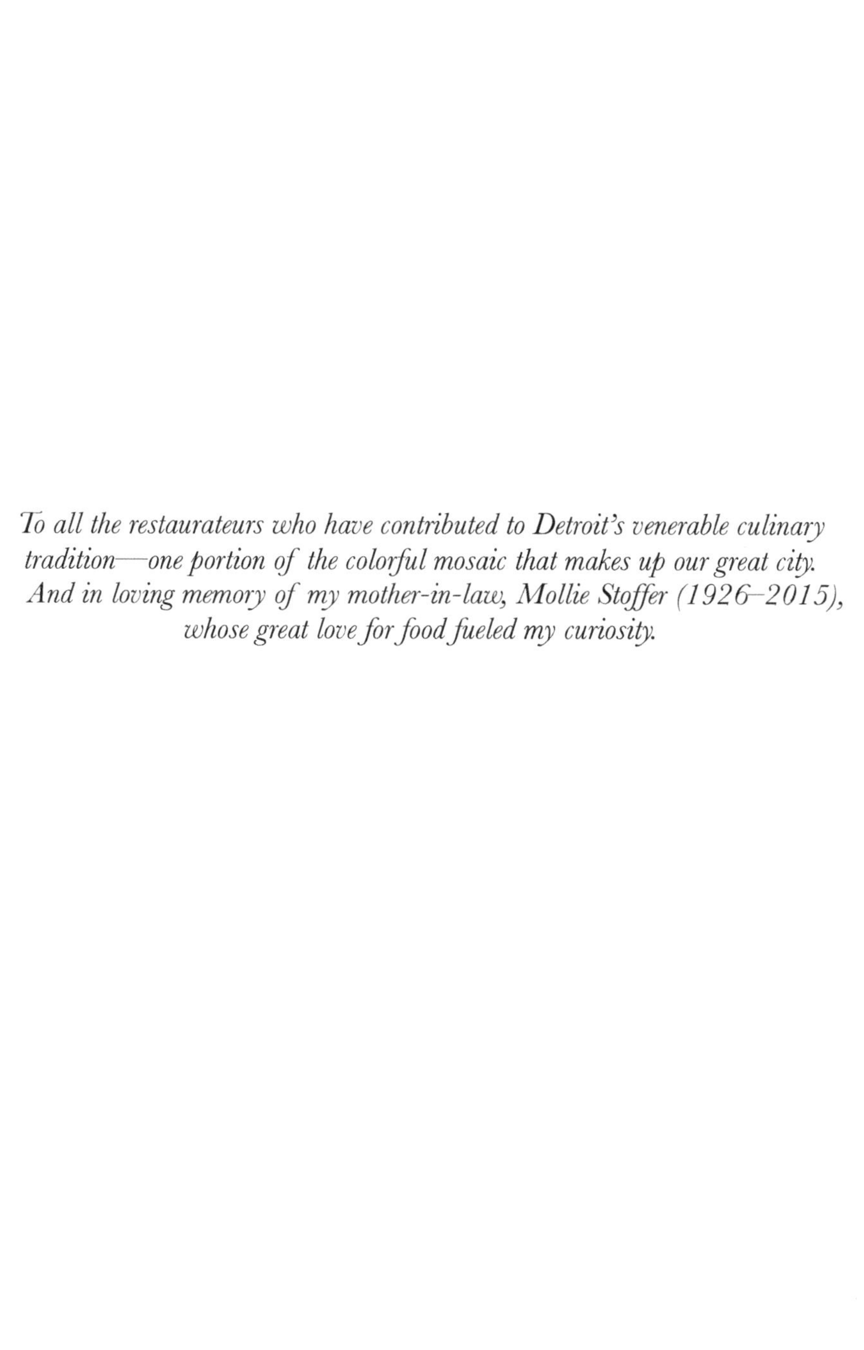

To all the restaurateurs who have contributed to Detroit's venerable culinary tradition—one portion of the colorful mosaic that makes up our great city. And in loving memory of my mother-in-law, Mollie Stoffer (1926–2015), whose great love for food fueled my curiosity.

Contents

Contents

Acknowledgements

As an author, I always feel obliged to first recognize the one person whose help was the *most* indispensable. My very special thanks go to my editor, Krista Slavicek, whose patience, thoroughness and expert guidance helped me with myriad issues during the past several months.

Just as no restaurant can operate without patrons or staff, no author can assemble a book without sources. Throughout this time-consuming process, I've been helped by numerous people, those with an intimate knowledge of the Detroit's dining scene—both past and present—and by several librarians, archivists and journalists.

My sincere gratitude goes to Detroit restaurateurs Connie Bacigalupo, Janet Sossi Belcoure, Tom Brady, Tommy Burelle, Grace Keros, Patrick Liebler, Wesley Pikula, Justin Vesper and Joe Vicari.

My thanks also go to Molly Abraham, longtime Detroit restaurant critic; Mark Bowden and the staff of the Burton Historical Collection of the Detroit Public Library; Richard Bulleri; Stephanie Angelyn Casola of Franco Public Relations; Elizabeth Murray Clemens and Mary Wallace of the Walter P. Reuther Library of Urban and Labor Affairs at Wayne State University; Michael Hauser; Michael Jackman of the *Detroit Metro Times*; Charlie Langton of WJBK-TV, Fox 2; Arnold and Shirley Silverman; and my cousins Lynn, Marshall and Scott Shencopp.

My deep appreciation goes to my wife, Sheryl, and to our son, Evan, for providing me with interesting ideas, lending their support and offering me encouragement in my occasional moments of frustration.

Thanks are also due to my friends Nancy Hand and Karin Risko, who helped me with obtaining images and directing me to sources.

Introduction

I was at this restaurant. The sign said "Breakfast Anytime."
So I ordered French Toast in the Renaissance.
—Steven Wright

Time travel aside, Detroit's long culinary tradition begins with the contributions of the French and dates almost as far back as the Renaissance. Over the intervening decades and centuries, scores of other ethnic groups have made Detroit home, making their cultures their everlasting legacy to the city.

Style of cuisine represents just one aspect of a given group's contribution. Unique expressions of music and dance, sacred celebrations of holidays and traditional types of dress all underscore the ubiquity of Detroit's varied ethnic groups. The migration (and integration) of the population during the postwar years has allowed the greater community to appreciate this diversity. In metro Detroit, you can visit a jazz club featuring African American artists on the west side, take in a museum dedicated to the contributions of Arab Americans in Dearborn or attend a Cinco de Mayo festival in Mexicantown.

But a special pride is reflected in a group's food traditions. Food serves as an intimate window into the culture of a people—and by extension, an ethnic restaurant represents that culture's outreach to the greater community. For restaurateurs, business has a twofold purpose: providing a livelihood while extending their group's unique hospitality to the public.

Immigration to the Detroit area in recent decades has only added to the assemblage of ethnic groups represented in southeast Michigan, and most, if not all, offer their unique cuisine to the public in their traditional manner. So, in addition to finding French duck charcuterie at Cuisine, Polish kielbasa at the Ivanhoe Café, German knackwurst at the Dakota Inn Rathskeller, Italian escargots à la Bourguignonne at the Roma Café or authentic Coney dogs at American Coney Island, you'll be able to enjoy creations presented by the Vietnamese, Cuban, Indian, Jewish, Ethiopian, Irish, Guatemalan, Greek, Arabic, Chinese and Japanese communities—to name only a few. In addition, a nucleus of "American"-style restaurants featuring dishes that are often a fusion of French, German and Italian traditions stand as a mainstay of Detroit's dining scene. Some are very upscale, reflecting the wealth brought to the area by the automotive industry.

As the twentieth century progressed, and the restaurant scene in Detroit grew more influential, a few establishments accomplished an especially rare feat and actually *invented* a food or beverage within their walls. The ubiquitous Coney dog? It's something you can find now at almost any suburban intersection, but it all began with American and Lafayette Coney Island in the heart of downtown, where Michigan Avenue, Lafayette Boulevard and Griswold Street converge. Detroit-style deep-dish pizza owes its origins to the original Buddy's at Conant Avenue and Six Mile Road. The interesting concoction of red wine and champagne known as Cold Duck was born at the Pontchartrain Wine Cellars on Larned Street. And the delightfully inebriating beverage known as the Hummer—a combination of Kahlúa and rum blended with vanilla ice cream and ice—was conceived and first formulated in 1968 by Jerome Adams, a bartender at the Bayview Yacht Club, perched on the banks of the Detroit River.

The ingenuity behind these accomplishments speaks to the originality present in the Detroit area. Often seen as a place responsible only for cars, southeast Michigan is home to many other innovations of culinary creativity. Others include achievements in finance, advertising, medicine and the fine arts.

Yet in Detroit, as in virtually any major American city, the passage of time begets inevitable change. Populations shift, leading to the dissolution of previously homogenous neighborhoods. Consumer tastes change, especially in the media-driven twenty-first century. And independent restaurateurs often discover a lack of interest among their children in taking over the family business. As such, many restaurants—some of which once enjoyed strong followings—closed their doors as the decades marched on. It can be argued that these winds of change hit Detroit much harder than other American cities. Urban experts have advanced theories, but the most likely candidate might just be the invention that led to the rise of the city: the automobile and the boundless mobility it encouraged.

Success in the restaurant business is a unique challenge requiring special skills that build legacies and create generations of precious memories. In a 2007 article in *HOUR Detroit*, local food critic Christopher Cook explained how a restaurant differs from almost any other type of commercial establishment:

> *Restaurants have personalities, just like people. They run the gamut from the steady community anchor, to the ditzy passing fad, to the dysfunctional flop. Those that succeed do so because they change little when they do something well, and continuity and consistency are measured in years rather than months. They are the steady places to which we like to return to be reminded that when all else seems out of whack, some things don't change.*

This book pays tribute to these storied institutions and seeks to rekindle warm memories of dining in yesterday's Detroit. While some existing venues are included, the great majority of the text shares the stories of the defunct eateries—and a few watering holes—of the past, places many locals will find familiar. As singer Joni Mitchell so eloquently states in her hit song "Big Yellow Taxi," it's true that "you don't know what you've got 'til it's gone." All too often when a longtime restaurant closes, former regulars might think, "Wow, since I moved to the other side of town, I lost track of that place. Too bad it's not going to be there anymore." Such a realization often conveys a sadness that part of the city will never again be quite the same.

It is worth recognizing, however, that while the closing of a storied restaurant is a loss for the community, new places to eat continue to open. Some meet an early fate, but others survive and usher in new traditions for Detroit to embrace.

Although these departed restaurants are no longer with us, their years spent as community fixtures reside in our common memory and continue to define our city today. This author's hope is that these recollections will resonate among a vast swath of diners in southeast Michigan—Detroiters all.

Part I

Bistros and Cafés: Detroit's Legacy of Fine Dining

A sad truth lies in the fact that Detroit, as a city, has long suffered from a national inferiority complex—at least when it comes to fine dining. Lacking the glamor of a New York or San Francisco or the trendiness of a Los Angeles or Miami, the city is too often relegated to the national backwater, the fairness of which seems questionable. The late Elmore Leonard, the famous novelist and screenwriter, offered a telling insight on Detroit when he wrote:

> *There are cities that get by on their good looks, offer climate and scenery, views of mountains or oceans, rockbound or with palm trees; and there are cities like Detroit that have to work for a living, whose reason for being might be geographical but whose growth is based on industry, jobs. Detroit has its natural attractions: lakes all over the place, an abundance of trees and four distinct seasons for those who like variety in their weather, everything but hurricanes and earthquakes. But it's never been the kind of city people visit and fall in love with because of its charm or think, gee, wouldn't this be a nice place to live.*

Because of this second-string reputation, the national presumption was that restaurants in Detroit—even at its mid-twentieth-century zenith—were second tier and had little to offer. The truth, then and now, is actually quite different.

With the auto industry forming the cornerstone of the local business community, Detroit (which, by the 1950s, had grown to become the fourth-largest city in the nation) became blanketed with dozens of fine-dining establishments, serving a huge assemblage of executives, mid-managers and salespeople, not to mention lawyers, bankers and stockbrokers—the list is almost endless—some working directly in the car business and others in related fields, such as advertising, public relations and the like. Reading period newspaper reviews of these restaurants reveals the slower pace of the era, when fine dining was a leisurely but highly formal activity mainly aimed at the wealthy. Restaurants of this type were typically classic, understated old-world venues more numerous than their counterparts today. Present-day Detroiters under the age of fifty-five might be surprised to discover the markedly different tenor of that era—when strict dress codes were enforced, gender roles were rigidly defined and racial discrimination was practiced with little subtlety.

Given their tradition as rendezvous spots for the white-collared business community, many of Detroit's finer establishments clung to strictly formal customs and suffocating sexism. Even into the 1970s, Lester and Sam Gruber, owners of the London Chop House, would not seat unaccompanied women after 6:00 p.m. At the Caucus Club, women were excluded from sitting in the exclusive backroom until the late 1970s.

But over the next few decades, thousands of nonprofessionals who had become members of the middle class (a standard of living higher than mere subsistence, created by the labor movement) were also able to enjoy finer dining at some of Detroit's less stuffy establishments. In short, the indelible changes unleashed by Henry Ford placed Detroit on the national map (literally and figuratively), and all those people had to eat!

1

Continental Cuisine

The Harlequin Café

"It's comfortable and cosmopolitan," wrote longtime restaurant critic Molly Abraham in 1983. She was referring to the much-missed Harlequin Café, an über-urban dining spot that was a West Village fixture for over twenty years.

Housed on the first floor of the Parkstone Apartments on Agnes Street, the Harlequin occupied what had been an old-fashioned drugstore. Opened in 1983 by brothers Mindy and Balbir Ahluwalia, the bistro was one of a wave of new establishments that opened in the neighborhood at the time. Their aim was to be a catalyst for reviving the West Village by offering reasonably priced meals in a pleasant and urbane atmosphere.

Mahogany apothecary cabinets—previously used to house medicinal items—displayed elegant artwork and abutted the original marble-topped soda fountain, which found new life as the bar. Taken together, small, intimate details like these created a setting that made the Harlequin perhaps the most romantic restaurant in Detroit. The menu hewed close to a Continental style, with offerings like herb baked chicken, stuffed flounder, pork tenderloin and lamb chops. Desserts were especially decadent and included a mouthwatering praline cheesecake. In 1986, *GQ* magazine included the Harlequin on its list of the best fifty new restaurants in the nation.

In 1993, Sherman Sharpe purchased the restaurant and made the menu more upscale. A glowing 1997 review in the *New York Times* described his level of personal involvement as "Dinner as Theatre,"

> *Mr. Sharpe's descriptions alone serve as dinner theater, and diners are always charmed. There are usually 9 or 10 appetizers, like hollowed new potatoes filled with lumpfish caviar and, if you are lucky, an array of shiitake, porcini and a half-dozen other mushrooms with a delicious Madeira wine sauce.*

The whole setting—the dark wood, the elegantly set tables draped in white tablecloths and the quiet atmosphere provided a special dining experience unlike any other in Detroit. But running a profitable restaurant in an urban neighborhood is always a risky venture, and in 2006, the quaint café closed due to declining business.

But recent years have seen a revival of interest in the West Village. Apartment occupancies are up, real estate values are increasing and more pedestrians can be seen on the sidewalks. Restaurateurs have taken note, and in late 2013, a delightful new eatery, Craft Work, opened in the same location as the old Harlequin Café. Elegant yet unpretentious, Craft Work prides itself on serving "New American food" made from quality ingredients. More positive developments have followed, including a coffee shop and a nearby vegan diner. At this writing, these look to be the first of several setting up shop in this charming neighborhood.

LITTLE HARRY'S

"If walls could talk" is a phrase that so often prefaces a story about a historic place. The line may well be overused, but in the case of the Alexander Chene House, aka Little Harry's restaurant, it is well deserved. In fact, its historical significance predates even the construction of the house itself.

The house was built by the St. Onge family on land bequeathed by Louis XIV in 1707. The parcel was part of a system of "ribbon farms," which were long, narrow strips of land that ran perpendicular to the Detroit River and extended as much as a mile inland. According to a 1963 piece in the *Detroit Free Press*, Pierre St. Onge, the first member of the household in Detroit, soon acquired the nickname "Chene," which gradually morphed into the family surname.

After being constructed in the mid-nineteenth century, the home first served as a private residence. After being expanded, it served as a University of Detroit fraternity house, a blind pig during Prohibition

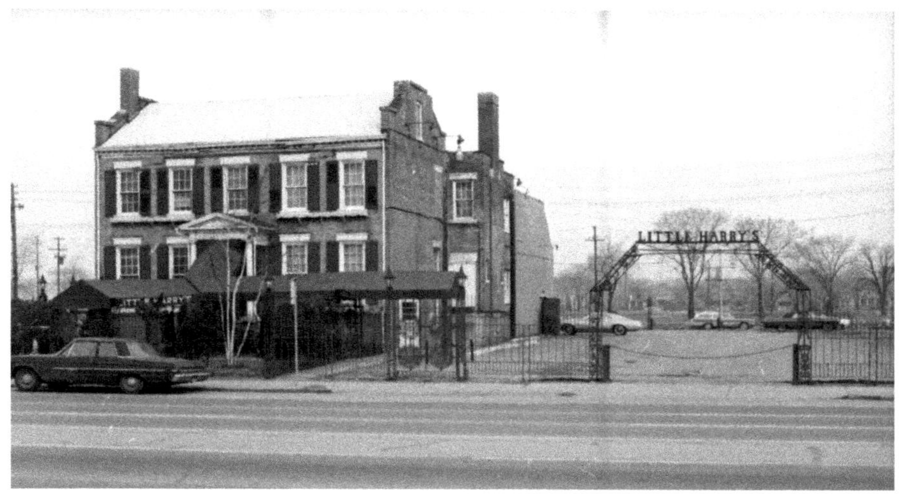

A view of the historic Alexander Chene House (aka Little Harry's restaurant), circa 1968. *Courtesy of the Walter Reuther Library.*

and, beginning in 1935, a fine-dining establishment. Restaurateur Harry Bianchini operated the business until 1958, when he sold it to Diamond Phillips. The menu featured classic American fare, with a 1947 edition listing perennial favorites, such as Lake Erie trout, broiled swordfish, roast prime rib and broiled lamb chops.

Under Phillips, the restaurant established a fiercely loyal clientele, whom he communicated with via an informal monthly newsletter, *Harry's Little News*. The paper provided news on new menu items, personal news in the lives of regular customers and updates on Phillips's recent travels.

Phillips was also very respectful of the building's long history. When doing renovations in 1958, he found a cache of letters (from an unknown sender) hidden inside of a wall. After discovering they were love letters of a very intimate nature, Phillips felt guilty for reading them, prompting his decision to burn the messages.

Even for those who didn't dine at Little Harry's, the building, as an example of nineteenth-century Federal-style architecture was a source of pride among historic preservationists. Hollywood took notice as well. Tommy Lee Jones and Jane Alexander appeared in a scene filmed in the dining room for the 1978 film *The Betsy*, the motion picture based on the novel of the same name by Harold Robbins.

But like many of the city's fine-dining establishments, Little Harry's met an unceremonious end—with an especially tragic twist. By the 1980s, many of the surrounding businesses, especially advertising agencies serving automotive clients, had migrated to the suburbs, decimating the restaurant's lunchtime trade. In 1990, Little Harry's closed, and Phillips sold the building to singer Anita Baker. At first, Baker and her husband stated they planned to convert the structure into a recording studio. Later they changed course, saying only that they planned a vaguely described "exciting development" without providing details. Soon, however, they announced their intention to demolish the former restaurant as a necessary part of their redevelopment.

Since the building was protected as a State of Michigan Historic Site, government approval would be required. After being denied permission by Detroit's Historic Review Board, the owners pursued the matter in court, where they prevailed. Local historic preservationists then obtained an injunction staying the demolition pending an appeal. But mysteriously, a demolition crew arrived the very next weekend and reduced the building to rubble. Baker later claimed no part in the illicit move, saying she was out of town and unaware of the events. Media investigations after the fact suggested possible political corruption as a factor.

The loss to the community from the demolition was doubly painful when the eventual outcome became known. The promised "exciting development" turned out to be anything but. Rather, a mundane-looking International House of Pancakes now occupies the site.

THE LONDON CHOP HOUSE

In the not too distant past, Detroit had a considerably different character than it does today, despite the city's recent rejuvenation. The coming of age of the auto industry produced a well-documented middle class but also spawned a small but burgeoning provincial aristocracy—high-level executives representing automakers, principle suppliers and advertising agencies, descendants of the industry's pioneers plus powerful local politicians and high-powered attorneys. This combined with the comparatively formal tone of the era gave rise to a number of top-tier establishments that catered to the wealthy and influential. Among these, the London Chop House clearly ranked at the top of the heap.

Opened in 1939 by brothers Lester and Sam Gruber, the Chop, as it was informally known, was envisioned as a place to "bring together the pleasures of eating and drinking and offering them in a warm atmosphere, reminiscent of Old World Inns," according to the greeting on its menu cover. Strenuous efforts were made to provide precisely that. Exotic (but very Old World–sounding) entrées, such as English mutton chop, fresh sturgeon steak roast and stuffed Long Island duckling, shared menu space with an extra-thick sirloin steak and broiled Lake Superior whitefish. Intriguing caricatures of local celebrities by artist Hy Vogel lined the walls. The wine cellar was recognized as one of the five best in America. In 1961, restaurant critic James Beard recognized the London Chop House as one of the nation's ten best restaurants. And despite the restaurant's high-powered image, one simple little gesture was always observed. When a customer who phoned in a reservation was seated, a book of matches and a dime were waiting on the table—the dime being reimbursement for the cost of the phone call.

A superior menu notwithstanding, money and power were the pillars that supported the Chop House. Regular patrons were usually seated in unofficially assigned booths, the desirability of each being indexed to the customer's social status. Legendary Booth No. 1 was usually reserved for Henry Ford II, Frank Sinatra or Barbra Streisand.

Not surprisingly, prices were stratospherically high. An old rumor was that the restaurant employed spies to visit competitors to scout their prices just to make sure the Chop House's were set the highest. But in 2009 a revelation made by food blogger Jan Whitaker proved rather surprising:

> *What strikes me from the vantage point of 2009, as I look at recipes and depictions of popular dishes at the Chop House, are both the food shortcuts employed and the richness of the ingredients used, characteristics which mark it as a mid-20th century American restaurant. It was typical of the times, I know, but it still surprises me that a restaurant with sky-high prices (easily running up to $50 a person for food alone in the 1970s) would bake carrots with "maple flavored" syrup, stir onion powder into mashed potatoes, and dissolve chicken bouillon granules into their watercress soup.*

By the 1980s, the tastes of Detroit's bourgeois changed as they embraced different lifestyles. Suburban migration and a growing fear of downtown cut deeply into the Chop House's business. Les Gruber sold the restaurant shortly before his death in 1981, and during the subsequent years, its decline accelerated. Renovations to the interior and the introduction of a healthier menu—aimed at attracting younger customers—failed to turn the tide. Despite a move by a group of prominent businesspeople to rescue the Chop House, its doors finally closed in 1991.

But the strength of the London Chop House brand never completely died. In 2012, a group of local investors capitalized on the remarkable resurgence of the downtown area. After buying the mothballed restaurant and embarking on a top-to-bottom restoration, the storied eatery reopened to a grateful Detroit. Despite the obvious good news, the optimism was tempered with an understandable degree of caution by the media. However, four years into its second life, the Chop House is still thriving, despite the arrival of new competitors.

In its new incarnation, the London Chop House strives to honor its heritage, displaying the elegance and opulence of the past. At the same time, the restaurant also caters to today's diner, offering a contemporary menu, quality entertainment and a well-stocked bar.

Beautifully restored wood paneling, an upstairs cigar lounge (an exception to the new Michigan law outlawing smoking in bars and restaurants) and the return of a phone booth *with a working phone* are examples. As an example of how much the beloved restaurant's return was welcome, scores of former patrons donated a storehouse of memorabilia salvaged from the original London Chop House, including matchbooks, lobster bibs and, most importantly, a number of Hy Vogel's caricature drawings.

The Whitney

The Whitney, perhaps the grande dame of Detroit dining, also sports a remarkable irony—it's history as a restaurant extends back a mere thirty years. The storied and sumptuous mansion dates, however, to the late nineteenth century. Given all this history, talking solely about its time as a restaurant almost seems an injustice.

A native of Massachusetts, a young David Whitney arrived in Detroit in 1857 to manage the procurement of hardwood trees for two East Coast lumber concerns. Eventually, Whitney became an independent businessman and invested his profits from the lumber industry in related industries, such as shipping and railroad transportation. While married to his second wife (who, curiously, was the sister of his first) and at her behest, Whitney decided to construct a home befitting the couple's high station in life at the corner of Woodward Avenue and Canfield Street, then a newly emerging, upscale residential neighborhood on the city's northern fringe.

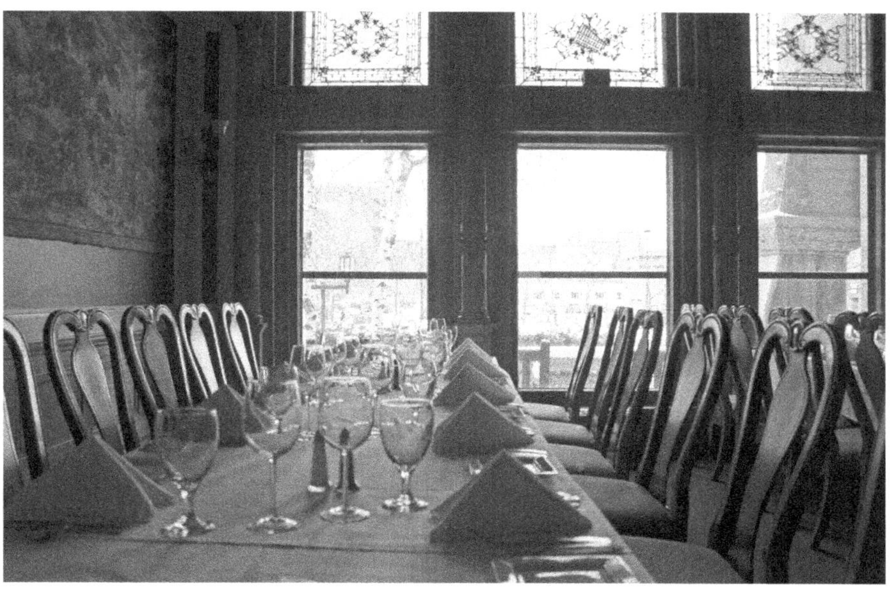

The elegant first-floor dining room at The Whitney awaits that evening's patrons. *Courtesy of the author, with thanks to Patrick Liebler.*

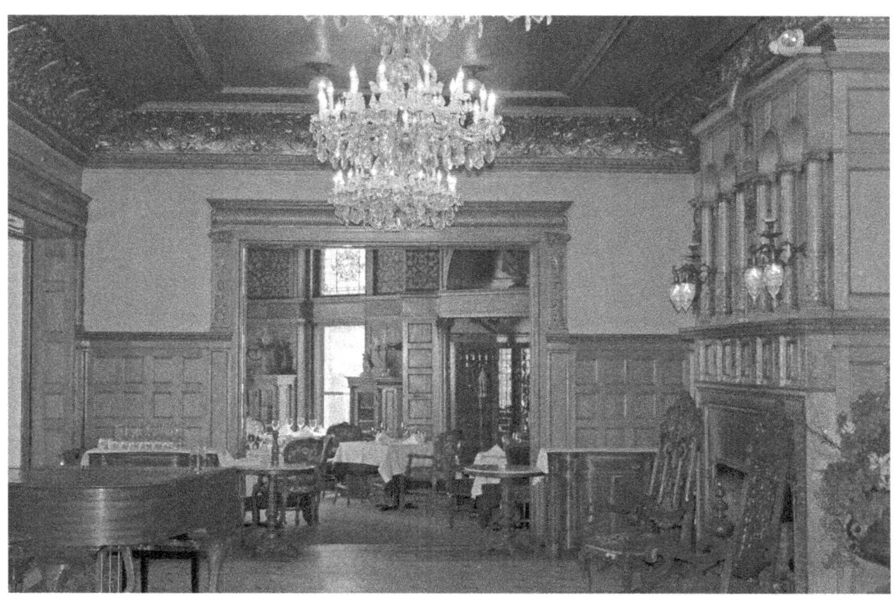

The stunning entrance hall at The Whitney echoes its past as the residence of one of Detroit's wealthiest citizens. *Courtesy of the author, with thanks to Patrick Liebler.*

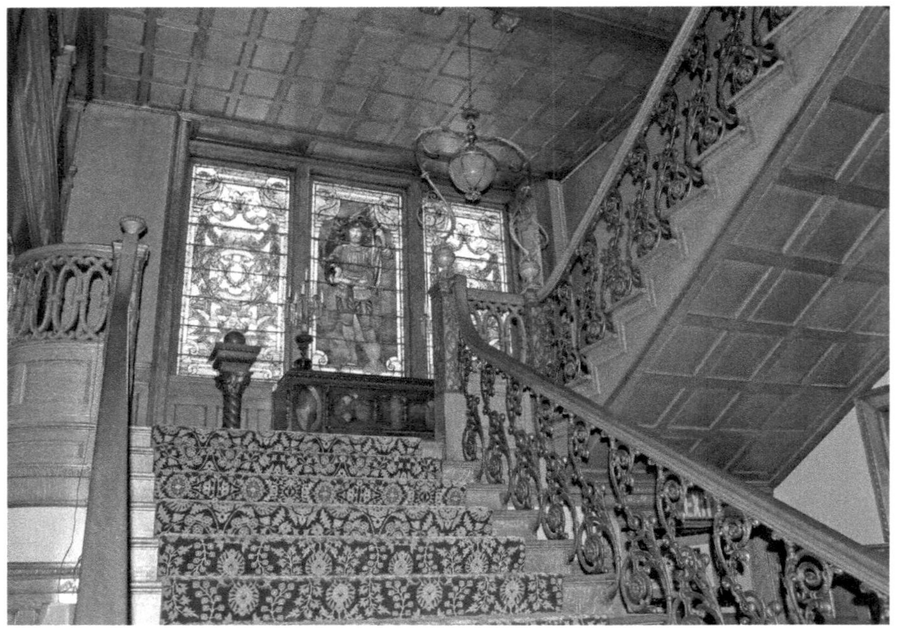

The staircase ascending to the second floor continues the Victorian motif. *Courtesy of the author, with thanks to Patrick Liebler.*

The mansion was designed by English architect Gordon Lloyd in 1894. According to architecture critic Eric Hill, the building "merged the Chateauesque with an attenuated Romanesque to create a unique, some would say awkward, expression." In addition to the Whitney mansion, Lloyd also designed Dowling Hall at the University of Detroit and Christ Church at Jefferson Avenue and Rivard Street, using similar techniques in those structures.

To say that the house is impressive would be a terrible understatement. The Whitney's website relates a few details of the amazing nature of the mansion:

> *Work began on the home in 1890. It was estimated to have cost $400,000 (about $9.5 million today) and was featured in several newspapers of the time. It was constructed using rose-colored South Dakota jasper, a type of granite. The Whitney mansion is 22,000 square feet and has 52 rooms (including 10 bathrooms), 218 windows, 20 fireplaces and numerous stained-glass windows crafted by Tiffany's of New York. It was the first residential home in Detroit to have an elevator for personal use, a hydraulic number. The Whitneys spent an additional $250,000 ($6.2 million*

today) on decorating and furnishing the home and another $300,000 ($7.5 million today) on artwork from around the world.

Four full years were required for construction, an understandable window of time when one discovers details of the building's over-engineered architecture. Hardwood floors were made two inches thick when a mere quarter inch would do. The concrete driveway was poured to a depth of eighteen inches, far in excess of the standard six. The extreme hardness of the rose jasper stone proved frustrating, forcing the tradesmen to constantly replace their blades and drills. The problem became so onerous that Whitney set up a temporary blacksmith shop on the site.

After the family moved in 1894, David Whitney devoted the third floor to displaying his personal art collection, consisting of pieces he purchased in New York and while traveling through Europe. The main floor featured several formal parlors, including a music room. The room derives its name from an invisible detail—the backing of the painting on silk mounted to the ceiling. Paintings on silk require a paper backing, and a common practice was to use discarded sheet music for this purpose because it was printed on the finest-quality paper of the era. Although unconfirmed, it's widely suspected that the musical staffs would still be visible were the painting to be removed. Other interior touches include Tiffany stained-glass windows and intricately hand-carved woodwork.

After Whitney died in 1900, his widow and children continued to reside there until 1920, when it was gifted to the Wayne County Medical Association, which eventually deeded it to the Michigan Visiting Nurses Association. Both groups used the house for office space. In 1979, Michigan businessman Richard Kughn purchased the mansion, and in the mid-1980s, he undertook an extensive, historically sympathetic restoration with the intention of establishing it as a fine-dining destination. False ceilings and makeshift drywall from the 1950s were removed to reveal ornate friezes and richly stained oak paneling.

The painstaking restoration and renovation culminated in 1986, when the Whitney formally opened to an eager community. Throughout the years it has maintained its reputation as a contemporary dining destination that includes old-world touches. During their visits, patrons are encouraged to explore the mansion. Often their first stop is the third-floor bar for a pre-dinner cocktail, followed by dinner on the main floor and finally by dessert on the second level. The dinner menu blends favorites like beef Wellington and filets with the unexpected—pan-roasted Scottish salmon or vegetarian risotto. The Whitney, however, is clearly a place where the diner will want to leave room for dessert. White chocolate strawberries, chocolate raspberry torte, bright lemon torte and the luscious list goes on. All the desserts are made in house by a dedicated pastry chef. So proud is the Whitney's management of the sweet offerings that it recently gave the second-floor dessert destination its own identity: the Katherine McGregor Dessert Parlor. Patrons who may have dined elsewhere can stop by for a special end to their evening.

Part of the excitement of dining at The Whitney is the festive atmosphere that can spontaneously pop up. This usually happens when a particular room is booked for a wedding reception, but word gets out that a bride is in the house. Non-wedding guests will often peek in and sometimes even join in the festivities, usually to the delight of the couple.

But no discussion of The Whitney is complete without mention of its most mysterious aspect—the alleged apparitions of paranormal spirits. Whether you are a believer or not, the stories are nonetheless intriguing. One such example is the night an employee observed an elderly gentleman as closing time neared. When the employee approached, the figure is said to have disappeared into the floor. Another is a bartender's chilling tale. While waiting on a patron, he noticed another couple entering a nearby parlor. After finishing, he went to approach the newcomers to offer his service, only to find the room empty. The disturbing experience proved to be one too many and prompted the employee to tender his resignation.

Management, fully aware of this curiosity, has humorously dubbed the third-floor bar the "Ghost Bar." Different theories abound, but perhaps the most likely recognizes the ghost as none other than David Whitney, who died in the house in 1900.

Over the years, numerous researchers who specialize in the paranormal have visited the mansion to investigate these and similar stories, bringing along a variety of instruments capable of measuring energy. One group ascertained that the third floor is not merely a haunt for ghosts but also the location of a "vortex"—a supernatural portal leading to an alternate dimension or a parallel universe—food for thought, certainly.

2

Food and Libations

Diamond Jim Brady's

Evolutions in dining tend to happen incrementally and inconspicuously. But after a while, seasoned diners can look back on a particular restaurateur's innovation and see how it marked the beginning of a new and welcome trend, be it related to a place's food, service or atmosphere. Diamond Jim Brady's, located near Seven Mile Road and Greenfield Avenue, embodied several examples of this. In 1954, Jim Brady opened his eponymous bar and grill that was unlike its peers. Up to that time, bars were known primarily as establishments for imbibing. "Bar food," as it was known, was mostly an afterthought and usually consisted of basic burgers, fries and onions rings.

Brady decided to try something different, perhaps owing to his new restaurant's location on Detroit's far northwest side, which, by 1954, had a very suburban feel and was seen as an up-and-coming area. Northland Center, just a mile away, opened the same year, making northwest Detroit and the inner-ring suburbs a prosperous middle-class area. Capitalizing on this, Brady introduced a menu featuring Delmonico steaks, shrimp cocktail, chili and clam chowder—an especially popular item on Fridays. Borrowing from his Celtic heritage, Brady also offered Irish coffee—a drink made from coffee, Irish whiskey, brown sugar and heavy cream. Booths and tables shared quarters with the traditional bar, creating a hybrid type of establishment. Unlike most other bar owners, Brady saw the food he served as a way to

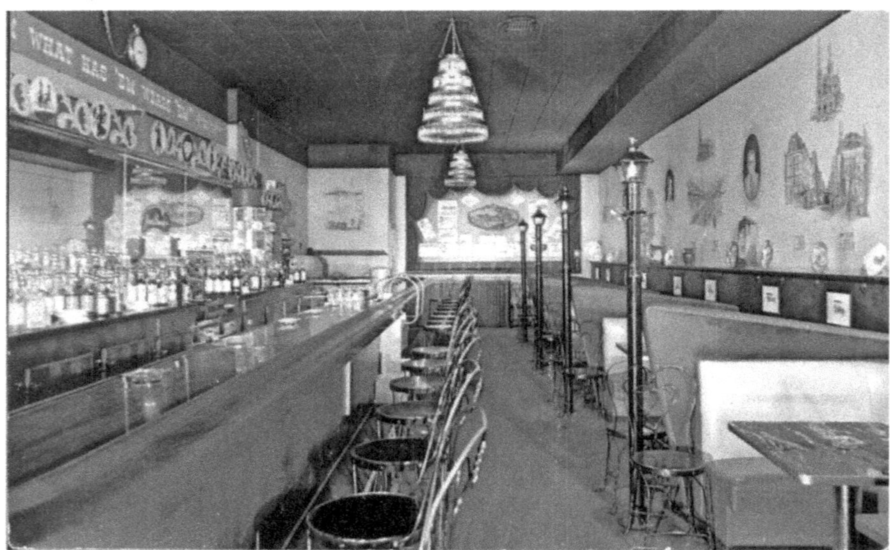

The cozy interior of Diamond Jim Brady's. *Courtesy of Tom Brady.*

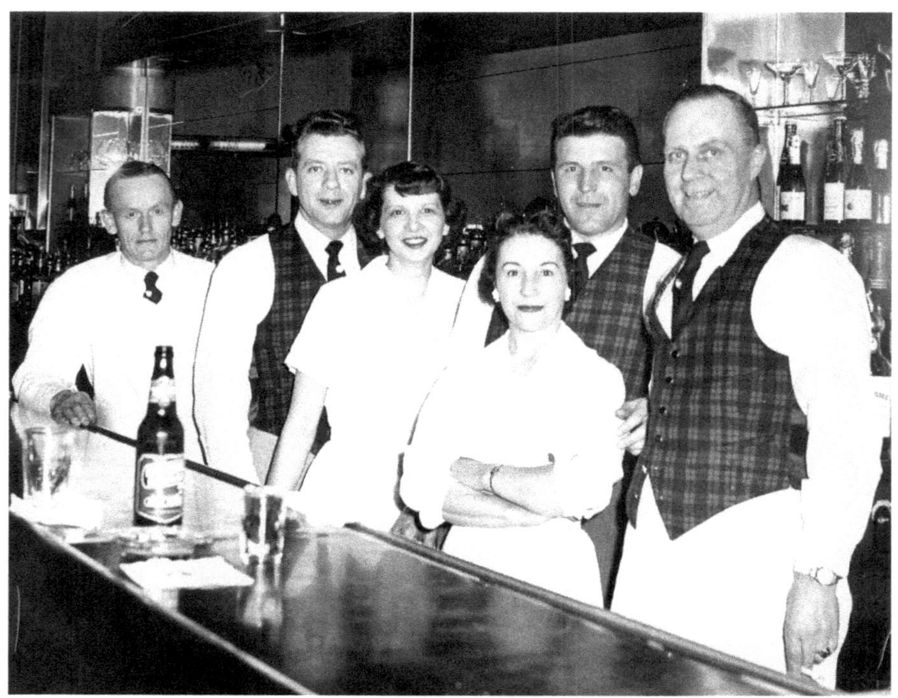

The original staff at Diamond Jim Brady's. *Courtesy of Tom Brady.*

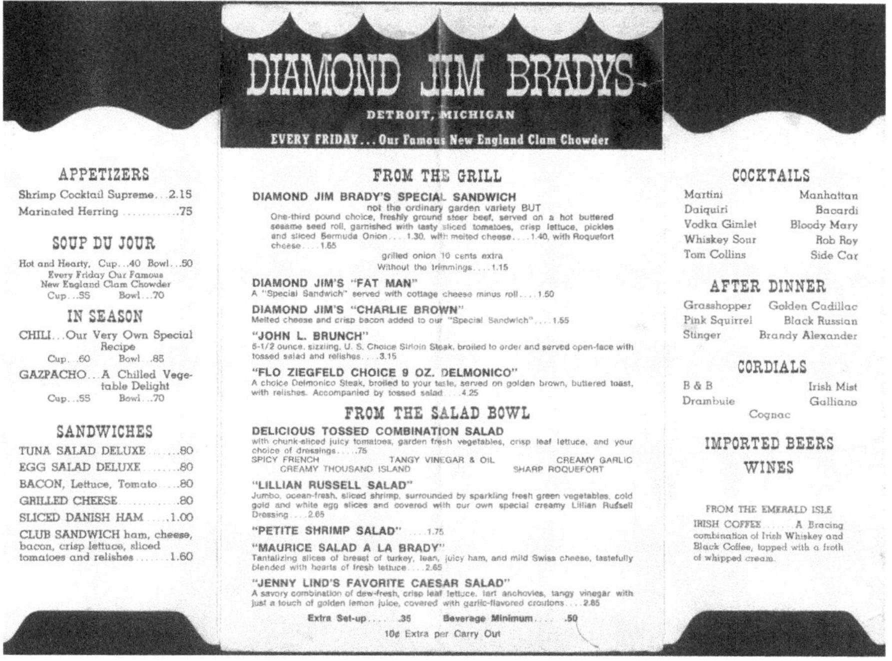

DIAMOND JIM BRADYS

DETROIT, MICHIGAN

EVERY FRIDAY... Our Famous New England Clam Chowder

APPETIZERS

Shrimp Cocktail Supreme... 2.15

Marinated Herring .... .75

SOUP DU JOUR

Hot and Hearty, Cup...40 Bowl...50

Every Friday Our Famous New England Clam Chowder

Cup...55 Bowl...70

IN SEASON

CHILI...Our Very Own Special Recipe

Cup...60 Bowl...85

GAZPACHO...A Chilled Vegetable Delight

Cup...55 Bowl...70

SANDWICHES

TUNA SALAD DELUXE 80

EGG SALAD DELUXE 80

BACON, Lettuce, Tomato 80

GRILLED CHEESE 80

SLICED DANISH HAM 1.00

CLUB SANDWICH ham, cheese, bacon, crisp lettuce, sliced tomatoes and relishes 1.60

FROM THE GRILL

DIAMOND JIM BRADY'S SPECIAL SANDWICH

not the ordinary garden variety BUT

One-third pound choice, freshly ground steer beef, served on a hot buttered sesame seed roll, garnished with tasty sliced tomatoes, crisp lettuce, pickles and sliced Bermuda Onion....1.30, with melted cheese....1.40, with Roquefort cheese....1.65

grilled onion 10 cents extra

Without the trimmings....1.15

DIAMOND JIM'S "FAT MAN"

A "Special Sandwich" served with cottage cheese minus roll....1.50

DIAMOND JIM'S "CHARLIE BROWN"

Melted cheese and crisp bacon added to our "Special Sandwich"....1.55

"JOHN L. BRUNCH"

5-1/2 ounce, sizzling, U. S. Choice Sirloin Steak, broiled to order and served open-face with tossed salad and relishes....3.15

"FLO ZIEGFELD CHOICE 9 OZ. DELMONICO"

A choice Delmonico Steak, broiled to your taste, served on golden brown, buttered toast, with relishes. Accompanied by tossed salad....4.25

FROM THE SALAD BOWL

DELICIOUS TOSSED COMBINATION SALAD

with chunk-sliced juicy tomatoes, garden fresh vegetables, crisp leaf lettuce, and your choice of dressings.....75

SPICY FRENCH TANGY VINEGAR & OIL CREAMY GARLIC

CREAMY THOUSAND ISLAND SHARP ROQUEFORT

"LILLIAN RUSSELL SALAD"

Jumbo, ocean-fresh, sliced shrimp, surrounded by sparkling fresh green vegetables, cold gold and white egg slices and covered with our own special creamy Lillian Russell Dressing....2.65

"PETITE SHRIMP SALAD" 1.75

"MAURICE SALAD A LA BRADY"

Tantalizing slices of breast of turkey, lean, juicy ham, and mild Swiss cheese, tastefully blended with hearts of fresh lettuce....2.65

"JENNY LIND'S FAVORITE CAESAR SALAD"

A savory combination of dew-fresh, crisp leaf lettuce, tart anchovies, tangy vinegar with just a touch of golden lemon juice, covered with garlic-flavored croutons....2.85

Extra Set-up.... .35 Beverage Minimum.... .50

10¢ Extra per Carry Out

COCKTAILS

Martini, Manhattan, Daiquiri, Bacardi, Vodka Gimlet, Bloody Mary, Whiskey Sour, Rob Roy, Tom Collins, Side Car

AFTER DINNER

Grasshopper, Golden Cadillac, Pink Squirrel, Black Russian, Stinger, Brandy Alexander

CORDIALS

B & B, Irish Mist, Drambuie, Galliano, Cognac

IMPORTED BEERS

WINES

FROM THE EMERALD ISLE

IRISH COFFEE ...... A Bracing combination of Irish Whiskey and Black Coffee, topped with a froth of whipped cream.

The menu at Diamond Jim Brady's circa 1954. Note the "Charlie Brown" sandwich. *Courtesy of Tom Brady.*

build loyalty among his regulars. He was often known to say, "I serve food for the convenience of my drinking customers."

Brady's enjoyed a regular clientele of neighborhood residents and businesspeople, as well as employees at nearby Sinai and Mount Carmel Hospitals. One reliable customer was Chuck Walton, whose visits were so frequent that Brady's decided to name a menu item after him, the "Charlie Brown"—a bacon and Swiss cheese burger.

Another interesting touch was provided with female patrons in mind. The ladies' restroom, outfitted with pink wallcoverings, included a desk with a courtesy phone. If a young lady found herself at the restaurant while on a "bad date," she could excuse herself, call her parents from the ladies' room and sneak out the back exit and into the alley when her transportation arrived.

Brady's son Jim Jr., eventually joined his father in the business and expanded the brand to the suburbs by opening a location in Southfield. As suburban expansion continued, a Novi location was added, which is run today by Jim Jr.'s wife, Mary. More recently, Jim Jr.'s son Tom Brady opened

Diamond Jim Brady's Detroit in Royal Oak. This newest location pays homage to its predecessor, featuring walls with vintage images of the Seven Mile and Greenfield site, reproductions of northwest Detroit street posts and a pink ladies' room.

At this writing, there are plans to return the Diamond Jim Brady's brand to the city of Detroit. Tom and his partners recently purchased the building on Cass Avenue and Peterboro Street, once home to Chung's Chinese restaurant. Once known as the notorious "Cass Corridor," the area is emerging as a high-energy entertainment district near the new Detroit Red Wings hockey arena. The new venue is expected to open in late 2017.

Jim's Garage

It might seem painfully obvious (at least to an outsider), but shouldn't a city spawned by the development of the automobile have at minimum one restaurant with an automotive theme? Well, during the 1968 model year, that's precisely what happened. Located in the basement of a nondescript building at Washington Boulevard and Larned Street, the place wasn't much from the outside. The décor inside was simple (wooden chairs, standard red carpeting and few wall hangings), but like a finely tuned sports car hiding a

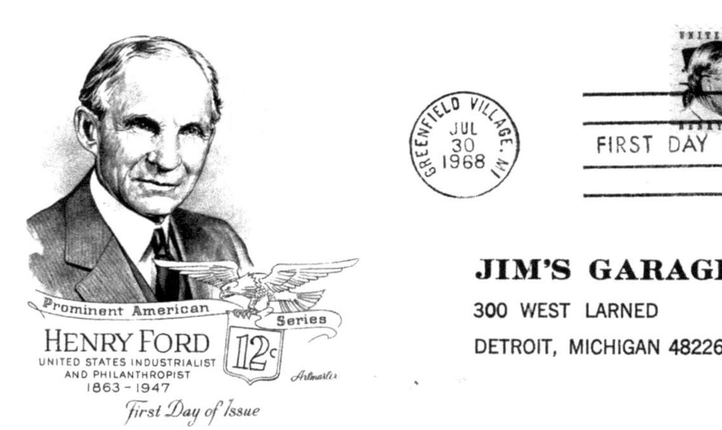

A letter sent from Greenfield Village to Jim's Garage with a first-day cancellation to celebrate the restaurant's opening. *Author's collection.*

souped up engine under its hood, the menu at Jim's Garage packed some serous horsepower.

Offerings tended toward seafood and included unusual entrées like filet of lemon sole, scampi danieli and a rare side dish called Anna potatoes—seasoned, thinly sliced potatoes, baked or fried in clarified butter until they achieve a cake-like consistency.

The menu itself reflected the automotive theme, with appetizers listed as "ignition," main courses as "fuel" and beverages as "lube." It all made for lots of fun.

But in 1985, the building housing Jim's Garage had to come down due to the expansion of Cobo Center just across the street. As of this writing, any efforts at opening another eatery in Detroit with an expressly automotive theme have stalled.

3
Seafood

Joe Muer's Seafood (Original)

Today, it's just an empty patch of land at Gratiot Avenue and East Vernor Street. But for most of the twentieth century, 2000 Gratiot Avenue was the home of Joe Muer's Seafood. Standing apart from the steady roster of steakhouses and supper clubs, Joes Muer's had the luxury of being without peer—the undisputed place in town for quality seafood.

But Joe Muer's emerged from fairly humble roots. In 1894, William Marburg, father-in-law of the original Joe Muer, purchased the building that until then had housed a grocery store. In 1906, Muer began to manufacture cigars on the site. The business flourished for over two decades before declining in the late 1920s. As a fallback, Muer decided to open an oyster bar in the building, which debuted on October 28, 1929—one day before the great stock market crash.

The operation was small at first—just a few tables and a handful of employees. But over the decades the building was continually modified to expand its capacity—first by Muer himself, then his son Joe Jr. and finally by Joe Muer III. By midcentury, the restaurant was known as the place for the very best in seafood—Boston scrod, Dover sole, East Coast flounder and Alaskan king crab. And there were always the familiar sides like creamed spinach and stewed tomatoes. But despite its notoriety, Muer's menu rarely strayed from the classics and stood as a testament to the "simple is best" philosophy.

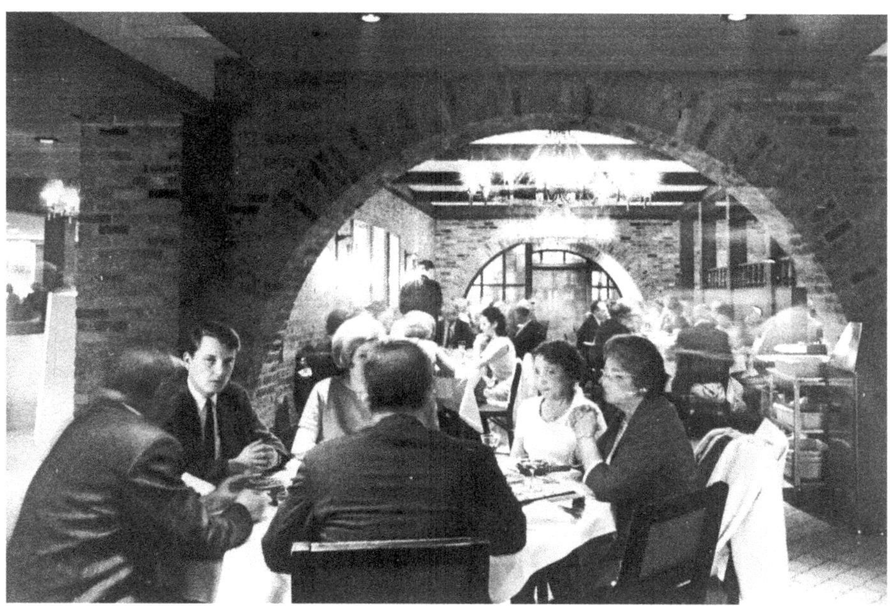

A view of the dining room at the original Joe Muer's Seafood on Gratiot Avenue. *Courtesy of the Walter Reuther Library.*

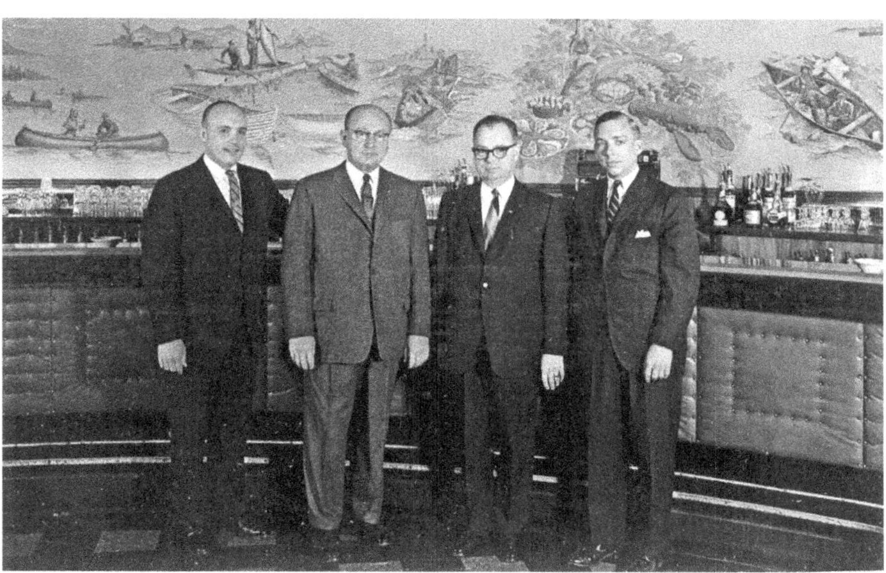

Postcard shot of the management staff at the original Joe Muer's circa 1968. Joe Muer III, instrumental in establishing the new restaurant, is at the far left. *Author's collection.*

For years, Joe Muer's was the backdrop for business entertaining, family celebrations and just about everything else. In a 2011 interview with the *Detroit Metro Times*, Joe Muer III said, "In the old days, people would make engineering drawings on tablecloths, write contracts on placemats. I witnessed the incorporation of a law firm. I had everything happen from engagements to marriages to divorces, from food-choking to death—everything except childbirth."

During the 1980s, Muer decided to open a satellite operation in Southfield, called Joe Muer's Grill. Outfitted with an Art Deco–style interior, the comfortable spot offered a menu similar to the downtown location, with an occasional experiment in creativity.

Because of its diverse clientele, Joe Muer's managed to weather the changing downtown restaurant scene better than many of its competitors. Gradually, however, the cumulative effect of departing businesses, the shrinking of its older clientele and increased levels of crime persuaded Joe Muer III to close the family business in 1998.

JOE MUER'S SEAFOOD (CURRENT)

Like a few other names in Detroit dining history, the mystique of Joe Muer's lived on long past its 1998 closure. In 2005, restaurateur Joe Vicari reached out to Joe Muer III, then in retirement. Together they discussed the possibility of reviving the Joe Muer's brand at a new location. The idea wasn't to exactly duplicate the original venue but to honor its traditions within the setting of a contemporary restaurant.

At the time, however, Detroit still suffered from the aftereffects of the problems responsible for Joe Muer's closing: an insufficient market. The idea was shelved at the time, but both men could see the trends beginning to reverse. In early 2011, the plan was put into action, which both Muer and Vicari saw as a positive contribution to the city's ongoing revival as much as a business venture. Muer agreed to lend his name and his culinary traditions to the project, which was located on the atrium floor of the Renaissance Center in the space formerly occupied by the Seldom Blues nightclub.

The result marries two eras in wonderful harmony. An oil painting of the original Joe Muer graces the entrance, and a reproduction of the original circular bar sits in the center of the main dining room. But a new feature—oversized windows offering sweeping view of the Detroit

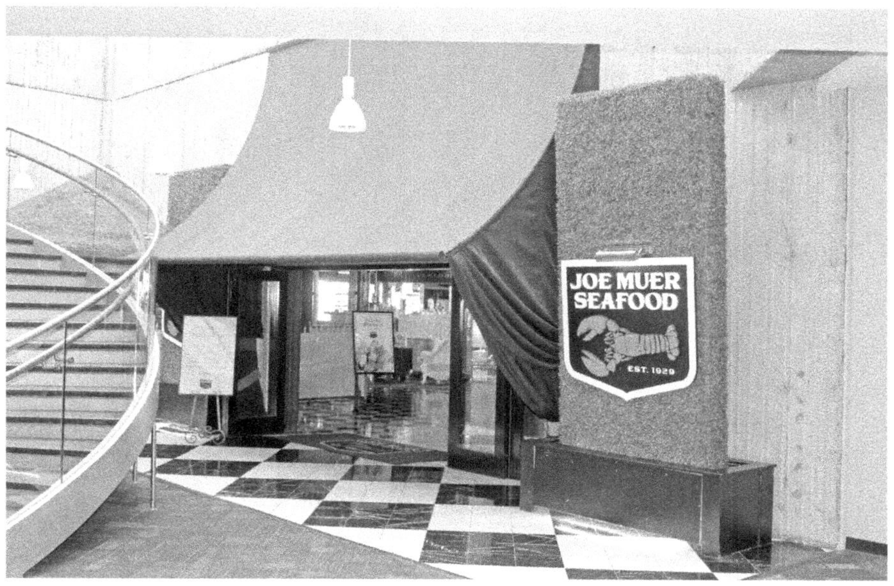

The entrance to the revived Joe Muer's Seafood at the Renaissance Center. *Courtesy of the author, with thanks to Joe Vicari.*

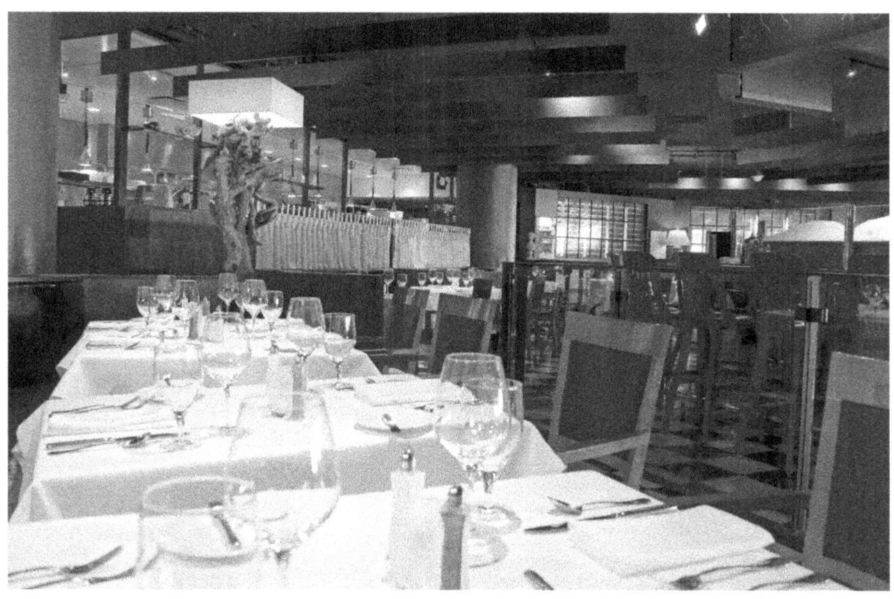

The stylish dining room at the new Joe Muer's. *Courtesy of the author, with thanks to Joe Vicari.*

River—offer a delightfully modern touch. New dishes that complement the classics, such as glazed Atlantic salmon and blue crab–stuffed shrimp, result in an updated but not radically new menu. The new Joe Muer's has been enthusiastically received, so much so that *HOUR Detroit* magazine honored it as its Restaurant of the Year in 2012.

In his article announcing the award, restaurant critic Christopher Cook pointed out the positive effect of Joe Muer's revival on the greater community.

> *In so many American cities, the pattern has been that once an icon like Joe Muer Seafood disappears it becomes part of the past, and that's it. So it says admirable and even remarkable things about the people willing to take a risk like this, and about the city, as well, when we see a figure of Muer's stature return. The signs are good. They point up, instead of down.*
>
> *Every big city needs a superb fish house. And in Detroit, we've got ours back. Joe Muer Seafood is a place to make everyone proud.*

4

Smorgasbord

Topinka's

It's certainly a confident restaurateur who is so convinced of his establishment's quality that he uses his name as the house moniker. It's even more impressive when, after the restaurant changes hands, the new owner retains the founder's name and hard-earned legacy.

Such was the path chosen by Ken Nicholson, who purchased Topinka's restaurant, then located at Baltimore and Hamilton Streets, from its namesake owner in 1947 and soon after moved it to West Grand Boulevard and Third Street. The restaurant did moderately well for the first several years, but following the conversion of the Fisher Theatre across the street to live entertainment in 1961, Topinka's business boomed.

Sporting a Swedish influence, an extensive smorgasbord was among the daily offerings. A 1962 review in the *AAA Motor News* mentions that it contained an eye-popping thirty-four items, including deviled eggs, caviar, cheeses and even peanut butter on crackers. Otherwise Topinka's was thoroughly American, with a menu featuring numerous seafood entrées, including perch, shrimp and scallops. Also featured were some unusual items, like turtle soup and roast duckling. Chicken, veal and steaks completed the picture—except for the libations. Topinka's flourished at a time when hard liquor was viewed as an essential element to a fine meal. Each of the two main dining rooms featured a generously sized bar, offering a steady stream of martinis, mojitos and cosmopolitans.

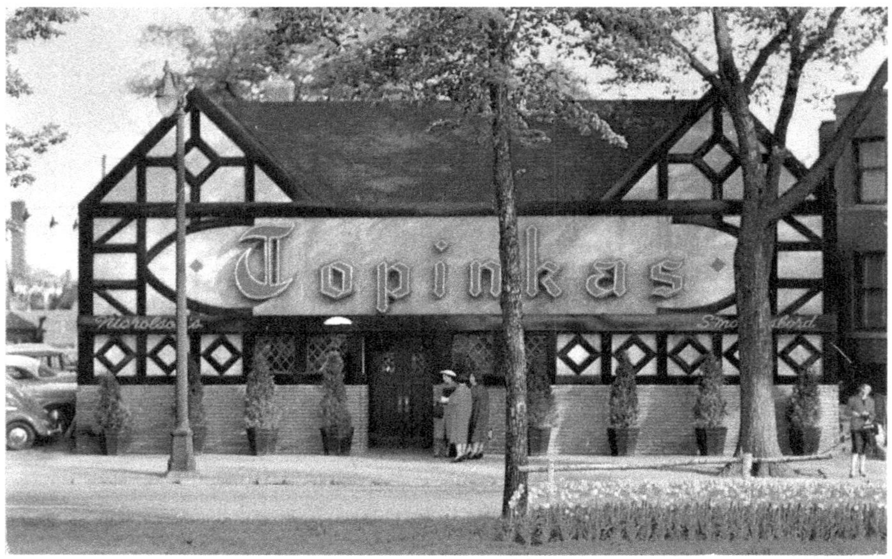

The original Topinka's on West Grand Boulevard—a popular dinner spot for a late dinner after a show at the Fisher Theatre. *Author's collection.*

Nicholson constantly looked for new innovations to introduce. A 1959 review in the *Detroit Times* shares a story about an out-of-town experience he had:

> *On a Florida vacation several years ago, Ken was smitten with the shrimp sauce at a restaurant. He approached the owner and, thinking they were both in the same club, asked him for the recipe. But this particular restauranteur knew a good thing when he had it and would not divulge the formula.*
>
> *Angry, Ken returned to his laboratory (kitchen) in Detroit and started to blend ingredients until he had finally just about duplicated the tasty sauce he discovered in Florida. And (wouldn't you know it) he now refuses to give out the recipe for this sauce.*

Topinka's prospered for decades on West Grand Boulevard. But as the 1980s merged into the 1990s, the crowd grew thin, resulting in its closure in 1995. A subsequent fire gutted the building, resulting in its eventual demolition.

TOPINKA'S COUNTRY HOUSE

A May 1959 *Detroit Times* review of Topinka's Country House is headlined "Topinka's Goes Suburban." At the time "suburban" meant no farther out than Telegraph and Seven Mile Roads—a point still within the Detroit city limits. But references to the location were just one feature harkening back to a bygone era. Another review in the *AAA Motor News* cites many of the restaurant's formal details, right down to the waiters' uniforms: "From its red and white striped, canopied doorway up stone steps, where water drips musically down a flagstone wall into shadowboxes, to the Fireside lounge set in a 'pit,' Topinka's exudes a feeling of a 'special evening' promising fine food to come....Waiters wear short red jackets with black trousers and ties."

So when Ken Nicholson decided to expand his Topinka's brand, he obviously spared no expense. Locating in a building that had previously housed a seafood establishment, this second Topinka's expertly duplicated the experience from West Grand Boulevard. Many of the same entrées were offered, along with classics like calf sweetbread, veal parmigiana and broiled snapper.

In addition to the self-explanatory Fireside Lounge, the restaurant offered rooms with romantic-sounding names, such as the Terrace Room and

Topinka's Country House on Telegraph Road was severely damaged by an early morning fire on January 5, 1972. *Courtesy of the Walter Reuther Library.*

Lamplighter Alley. Another bar, Cliffie's Saloon, paid tribute to Nicholson's one-time mentor, Cliff Bell, and bore a striking resemblance to Bell's eponymous bar/nightclub.

Topinka's flourished for several years on Telegraph Road, capitalizing on the population shift from the central city during the 1960s. A fire broke out during the early morning hours of January 6, 1972. When it was discovered several hours later, fire crews responded, but the building had already suffered considerable damage.

But Topinka's Road House was rebuilt and continued to serve the city for several more years. By 1989, however, business began to drop off, prompting its closure and ending the venue's long run.

5

Steakhouses

Carl's Chop House

Restaurants that evolve to become legendary local institutions often have humble beginnings. Carl's Chop House was a quintessential case in point. In 1932, World War I veteran Carl Rosenfield sat down for a night at the poker table. His opponent was his business partner, with whom he owned the Tiger Bar. At the end of the evening, Carl emerged as the sole owner of the bar, which he promptly sold. Soon after, he opened his eponymous steakhouse at Grand River and the John C. Lodge Freeway.

For decades, Carl's Chop House flourished as a popular lunch and dinner destination for businessmen, theatergoers and couples looking for a special night out. As the name suggests, red meat was what this restaurant was about—filet mignon, prime steer porterhouse for two, classic Delmonico—plus staples like pork chops, calf's liver and a variety of seafood entrées. In fact, a large lobster tank once dominated the view when diners first entered the lobby. Finding these choices elsewhere would have been easy, but at Carl's, quality set its food apart. An article in the *AAA Motor News* in 1962 explained how Rosenfield selected his meat:

> *Rosenfeld's meat comes from a herd of Black Angus cattle on his farm in Dexter, and he is proud that 25 years ago he started the practice of bidding high prices for winning 4-H Club cattle. It not only helped him get youth*

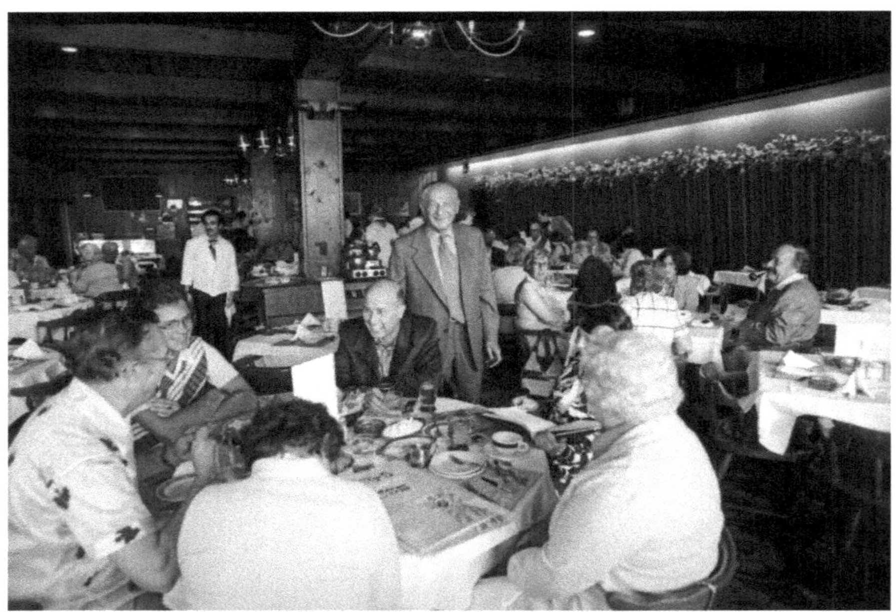

Carl Rosenfield was very much a hands-on restaurateur. Here he circulates among patrons at his legendary Carl's Chop House. *Courtesy of the Walter Reuther Library.*

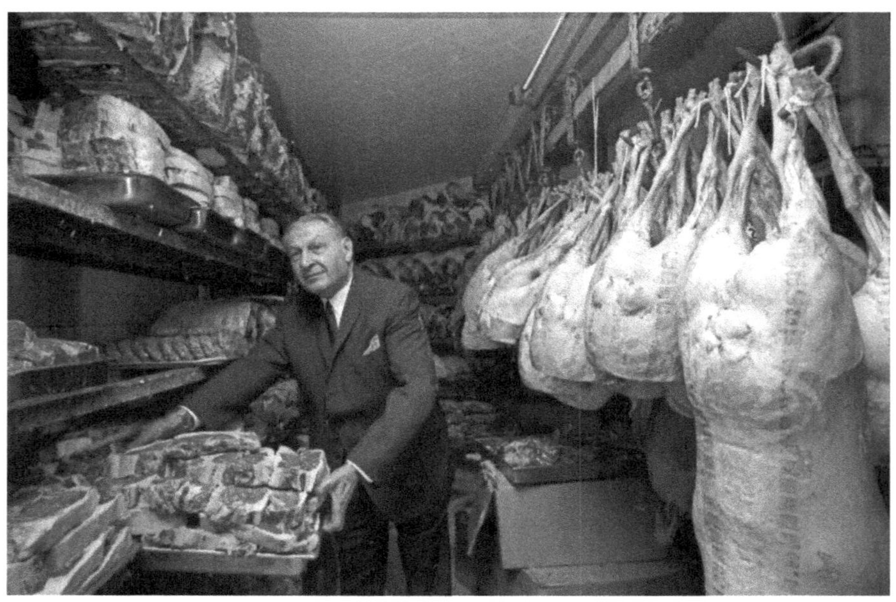

At Carl's, the menu was centered on generously cut steaks and prime rib. Here Rosenfield retrieves some of his inventory. *Courtesy of the Walter Reuther Library.*

started, but it furnished him another source for quality meats and hundreds of blue ribbons which he displays.

The emphasis on red meat was so strong that even the carpet featured illustrations of prime cattle. Menu prices from 1962 are more than enough to shock the modern diner. A full four-course meal could be had for as little as $2.75. Porterhouse for two? Just $11.00. And while many a culinary fad came and went at newer, trendier restaurants, Carl never wavered in his simple formula for success: meat or fish, baked potatoes or hash browns and a serving of steamed vegetables—and please try not to call them "veggies"!

But as the twentieth century progressed, the changing times were not kind to the chophouse. In 1990, Carl's was sold just as the downward spiral suffered by many downtown eateries hit high gear. Crowds thinned and then thinned some more when the gargantuan Motor City Casino opened just across Grand River Avenue. Would-be patrons found themselves drawn by the role of the dice and afterward satisfied their appetites at any of the casino's in-house eateries. The dearth in business forced the venerable establishment to finally close in 2008, with the building's demolition following two years later. Today, the site, like that of many of Detroit's storied institutions, is a nondescript vacant lot.

THE CAUCUS CLUB

Today, it's an empty corner in the otherwise stately Penobscot Building. Ensconced in the center of Detroit's financial district, the Caucus Club was opened by Lester and Sam Gruber in 1952 with an unusual mission: to handle the overflow from the storied London Chop House just across Congress Street. On especially busy days, the Chop House's enterprising owners might even send a patron to the Caucus Club to wait for a table at the London Chop House. The new spot quickly forged its own identity, offering signature drinks from its bar, including the Bullshot (beef broth, vodka and spice) and the Tom and Jerry (brandy with rum and meringue)

More sedate and simple than the status-obsessed London Chop House, the Caucus Club offered classic American fare: steaks, ribs and fish, including Dover sole and sautéed perch. But the restaurant's greatest legacy came from the role it played in music history.

In 1961, the Grubers booked an unknown singer from Brooklyn—nineteen-year-old Barbra Streisand, for her first gig outside her native New York. Despite the strong recommendation by her New York agent, the young singer did not initially inspire confidence. On his unauthorized website, Barbra Archives, biographer Matt Howe details the situation:

> *Ross Chapman, publicist for The Caucus Club remembered what he described as the near fiasco of hiring Streisand, "We told her she had four spots to do at the Caucus and she'd need at least 11 numbers. I asked how she was going to learn seven of eight numbers by nine that night—her first show. She looked me right in the eye and said, "I'm a fast learner." Matt* [Michaels, pianist] *rehearsed her until eight, when he had to go to work. He got her up to 10 songs. By the time she left Detroit, she knew 80 songs."*

Howe pointed out that this last claim might have been a publicist's exaggeration. But there's no doubt of Streisand's talent, as she demonstrated her awe-inspiring voice for weeks in the Caucus Club's backroom accompanied by Michaels on piano, consistently attracting sellout crowds while performing such popular songs as "A Sleepin' Bee" and "When the Sun Comes Out" by Harold Arlen and "Cry Me a River" by Arthur Hamilton.

During her stint in Detroit, Streisand was noticed by a talent scout who booked her on NBC's *Tonight Show* with Jack Parr. Working within the TV show's tight schedule, Streisand flew from Detroit to New York—her first time ever on an airplane, a fact that guest host Orson Bean made certain to point out. After returning to finish her engagement, the Grubers still promoted her show with "No Cover or Minimum Charge."

Streisand's initial contract called for her to perform three shows daily for a salary of $150 per week, less a 10 percent commission to her booking agency. After her return from New York, she sought to renegotiate her agreement. She asked for $250 per week plus meals. She was granted the raise but was denied her request for her meals.

Several regulars at the restaurant quickly took a liking to the young singer from Brooklyn and offered her assistance with housing and meals to augment her meager compensation. Over the ensuing decades, Streisand never forgot those who helped her so early in her career and always had prime seats reserved for her old friends whenever she did a show in Detroit. And as Streisand became famous over the years, the Caucus Club was quick to capitalize on the notoriety in its advertising. And from then on, pictures and memorabilia documenting Streisand's historic engagement adorned the walls.

By the dawn of the twenty-first century, Detroit, and the greater downtown area, was beginning its long climb up from decades of decline, reversing longtime trends and bringing people back downtown. But urban revivals can be jagged and uneven—often producing unexpected results. Despite increasing numbers of downtown workers and residents, dining at the beginning of the twenty-first century differed from the classic businessman's meals, a staple of the 1960s and 1970s for which the Caucus Club was known. In 2012, owner Mary Belloni made the difficult decision to close her restaurant after sixty years of service.

But hope does spring eternal—over the ensuing years, downtown's resurgence continued to gain steam, bringing even more residents and businesses while renewing some old traditions. At this writing, plans have been announced for a reopening of the Caucus Club in the near future.

Laffrey's Steaks on the Hearth

Sophisticated diners will often evaluate a restaurant by weighing a number of factors: the food, décor, service and price. Fans of Laffrey's Steaks on the Hearth tended to be more narrowly focused. For them, the ho-hum-looking bistro on West Seven Mile Road near Telegraph Road was *the* number-one place in Detroit to get a quality steak. From its opening in 1970, Laffrey's served a dedicated clientele made up largely of auto executives and local politicians. For these die-hard enthusiasts, the restaurant's local, independent status inspired their loyalty. As one online reviewer commented, "I am tired of people going to chains and saying how wonderful they are. If you live in Michigan, give money to people who have been here for years, not cheap copies of original restaurants in other cities. Laffrey's is a real Detroit steak house; it is my favorite place to go for steak."

And for decades Laffrey's enjoyed this loyalty. Corporate titans and individual diners looking for a good steak rubbed elbows with owners of small and medium west side businesses, traveling salesmen and high school prom-goers. What the plain Jane–style restaurant lacked in atmosphere it surely made up for in the quality of the food.

Unfortunately, the national chains eventually did arrive and leveraged their size to offer pricing that its independent neighbor couldn't match. After the holiday season in 2009, the west side steakhouse closed, taking a piece of local tradition along with it.

The Summit

Ever since it was constructed in the 1970s, the stunningly beautiful Renaissance Center on Detroit's riverfront has represented an optimistic hope for the future. Its Modernist architecture has been consistently renewed with renovations large and small—particularly the ambitious one undertaken by General Motors Company in the years after purchasing the complex as its new headquarters in 1996.

But even a place so seemingly new—despite now being nearly forty years old—can retain memories of days past. For many Detroiters, the legendary Summit restaurant is one example.

The Summit was a steakhouse restaurant located at the top of the center's rounded hotel tower, originally called the Detroit Plaza. Perched seventy-three stories above street level, the bistro was paired with a cocktail lounge one floor above. Both offered panoramic views of southeast Michigan and southwest Ontario. On an especially clear day, it was possible to see past Pontiac to the north and well past Windsor to the south.

But the real quirky thing about the Summit was its ability to rotate, offering diners a continuously changing landscape to peer out at. The cocktail lounge also rotated but at a slightly quicker pace than the dining room. The problem, however, was the fact that only the outer ring where customers were seated moved. The inner core, which included the kitchen and restrooms, remained stationary. Patrons would often emerge from the facilities turned around and confused.

Aside from the exceptional surroundings, the Summit offered a pleasant dining experience. Over time, the pure steakhouse menu was modified to include various seafood entrées. Each table was presented with a bucket of unpeeled shrimp after being seated, which proved quite popular. While waiting for their food, patrons loved working the shrimp meat out of its shell.

By the early 1990s, the Renaissance Center began to experience financial difficulties. Soon after the Westin Company, operator of the hotel, pulled out, and the Summit was closed. But GM's subsequent purchase of the center proved to be a game changer. Along with its planned rejuvenation, Marriott signed on as the hotel's new operator, and the automaker announced a revival of the top-floor restaurant. After a lengthy renovation, a new venue, Coach Insignia, opened in the same space. Coach Insignia—with seafood offerings like prosciutto-wrapped sturgeon and short rib ragout pappardelle—offers a more eclectic menu than did the Summit. Sporting a theme that celebrates the earliest era of the automobile, the new restaurant features paintings of

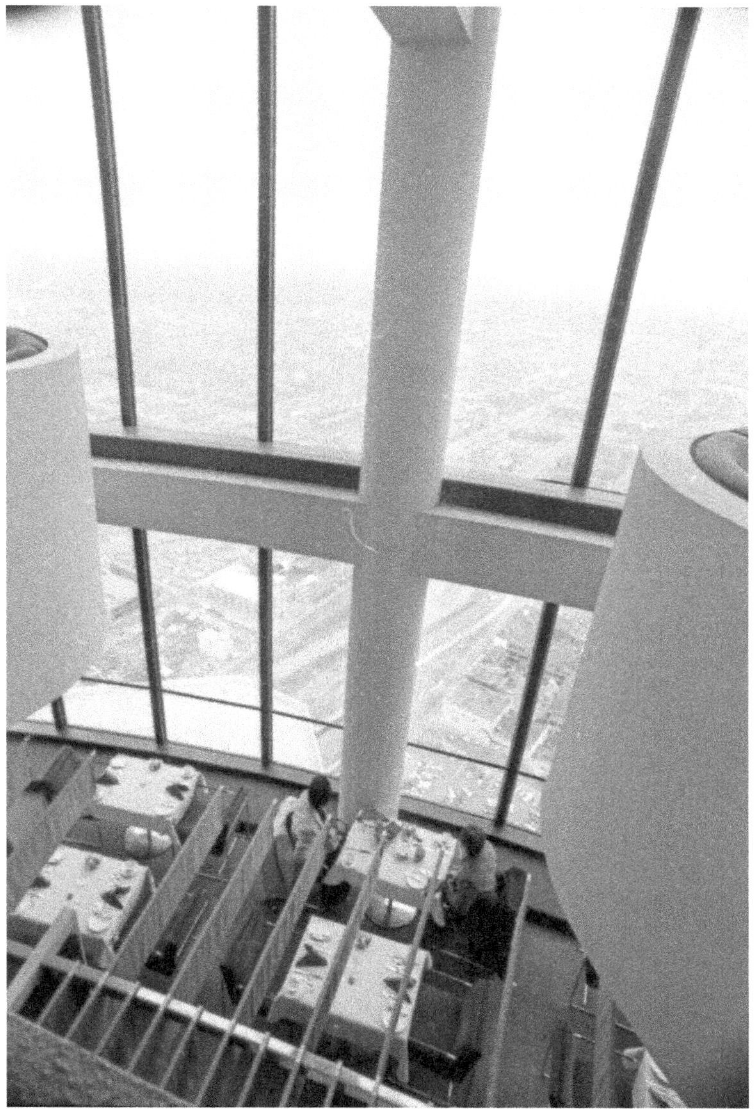

The Summit was a truly breathtaking place to dine—except for those fearful of heights. *Courtesy of the Walter Reuther Library.*

some of the finely crafted coaches built by the Fisher Body Company, which eventually became part of General Motors. Like its predecessor, Coach Insignia offers a stellar dining experience—but alas, the restaurant no longer rotates!

6

Traditional American

Machus Red Fox

Perhaps one of the greatest injustices done to the legacy of a fine restaurant is when it becomes famous (or infamous) for a reason wholly unrelated to what a dining establishment is supposed to be about—the ambiance, the service and, of course, the food. The Machus Red Fox in Bloomfield Township, perhaps the perfect example of the classic American upscale bistro, suffered this fate—perhaps more harshly than any restaurant in the United States.

On Wednesday, July 30, 1975, the restaurant's place in history was sealed. It was on that day that Jimmy Hoffa, former president of the International Brotherhood of Teamsters, arrived for what he believed was to be a reconciliation meeting with local mob figure Anthony Giacalone and New Jersey Teamsters official Anthony Provenzano; Hoffa had long-standing feuds with both men. After waiting in the parking lot for a time, Hoffa called his wife from a nearby payphone, saying that he had been stood up and was returning home. Hoffa was never seen or heard from again. Giacalone and Provenzano denied such a meeting was ever planned. The ensuing investigation involved federal, state and local authorities and was active for years. The case remains unsolved and is still officially open today.

The union leader was long known for his legal troubles and his associations with organized crime figures. In 1964, Hoffa was convicted in two separate trials held in U.S. District Court of fraud and jury tampering. After a series of unsuccessful appeals, he finally entered prison in 1967. In

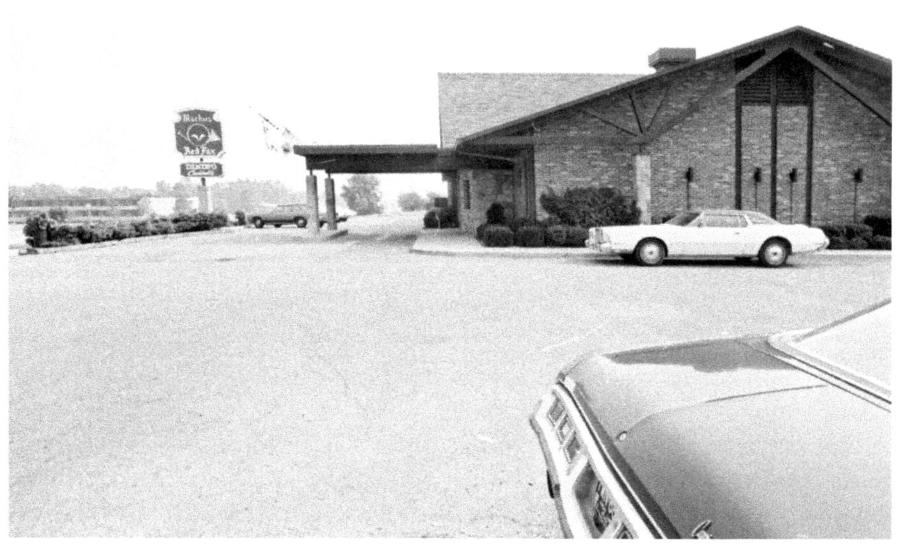

Exterior view of the Machus Red Fox—a restaurant that became infamous for an unintended reason. *Courtesy of the Walter Reuther Library.*

1971, President Richard Nixon commuted his thirteen-year sentence to time served, with the proviso that he abstain from any involvement in union politics until 1980, his originally scheduled release date. Displeased with this condition, Hoffa began legal action to circumvent it.

The reasons for Hoffa's presumed abduction and murder are unknown, but speculation suggests a desire by organized crime figures to prevent him from regaining the Teamsters presidency.

In the decades since, the FBI has occasionally acted on tips and conducted digs for Hoffa's body, mostly in various southeast Michigan locations. To date, none has proven fruitful. Despite the considerable number of years since his disappearance, speculation about Hoffa's fate remains a long-standing parlor game among many Americans, particularly in the Detroit area.

Throughout all of this, the name of the Machus Red Fox has been an omnipresent footnote. Unfortunately, the infamous event eclipsed many memories of the restaurant itself. Machus Red Fox was known for years as the quintessential patrician eatery and the community gathering spot for the wealthy residents of Bloomfield Township. Timeless American classics—thick steaks, expertly broiled fish entrées and elaborate salads, all prepared from the very finest ingredients—retained their popularity with local residents and businessmen for decades.

Amid its complex legacy, the Machus Red Fox shares one other connection to the Hoffa family. When Hoffa's son (and current Teamsters president), James Jr., married his wife, Virginia, in 1969, the Red Fox hosted the wedding reception.

STOUFFER'S DOWNTOWN

Rarely do national chain restaurants make a memorable impression on a community, but the Detroit-area locations of Stouffer's proved to be the exception. Founded by Abraham and Lena Stouffer in 1922 with a single restaurant in Cleveland, one of the company's first expansions was to Detroit, where it opened on Woodward Avenue at Campus Martius in 1929. Later, Stouffer's locations sprang up in a number of major U.S. cities, including New York, Chicago and Pittsburgh. Eventually, the company diversified into hotels and a highly recognizable line of frozen entrées.

Stouffer's always seemed to hit the right notes by offering a menu that was appealing yet affordable, sophisticated but unpretentious. Grilled lean lamb chops, poached eastern salmon hollandaise and sesame fried chicken

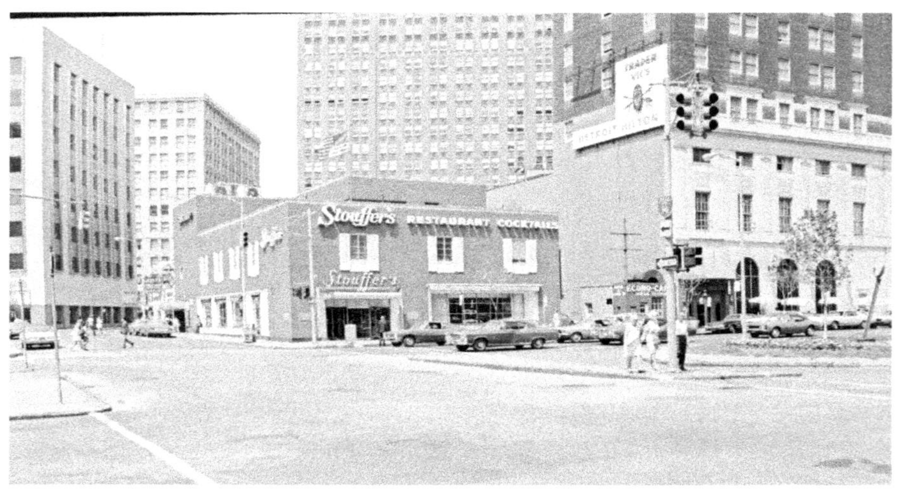

Stouffer's on Washington Boulevard. The restaurant's central downtown location contributed to its success. *Courtesy of the Walter Reuther Library.*

with grape preserves were just a few examples of Stouffer's creative legacy. Detroit was an especially successful place for the Stouffers, which prompted them to offer a second location on Washington Boulevard in 1935.

The company was so committed to quality that it even has its own in-house school to teach dietetics. In her memoir, *On My Own*, longtime Detroiter Many Demassa recounts her experiences:

> *At that time* [1955] *Stouffer's was very well thought of by dieticians for several reasons. Most importantly they offered a Dietetic Internship to qualified graduates at their headquarters in Cleveland. This was an administrative course that provided teaching in management Dietetics, including subjects such as equipment, recipes, purchasing, quality food preparation and personnel supervision. Stouffer's Restaurants had special attributes important to dieticians, such as accurate portioning, standardized recipes and accurate food purchasing.*

As the years wore on, however, Stouffer's met the same fate as many of its downtown counterparts—lack of business due to the outflow of residents and businesses to the suburbs. By the mid-1970s, both venues had closed, leaving yet another hole in the downtown dining scene.

STOUFFER'S EASTLAND

The considerable prosperity of the early postwar years brought wealth and upscale living to the inner-ring suburbs. Stouffer's decided to capitalize on this by opening two locations outside the city limits adjoining the new retail developments of the J.L. Hudson Company, Northland Center in Southfield and Eastland Center in Harper Woods.

Although shopping was entering the suburbs, at the time, it was still seen as the rather formal and time-consuming activity it had been downtown, requiring women to wear dresses and heels and men to be attired in coats and ties. Enjoying lunch in an elegant setting was often seen as an extension of this atmosphere. Both restaurants thus exuded a similar atmosphere, intending to attract shoppers from the exciting, brand-new retail venues nearby. The Eastland location hewed especially close to this theme. Echoing the nearby presence of the affluent community of Grosse Pointe, the free-standing building featured early American–style dining rooms and a

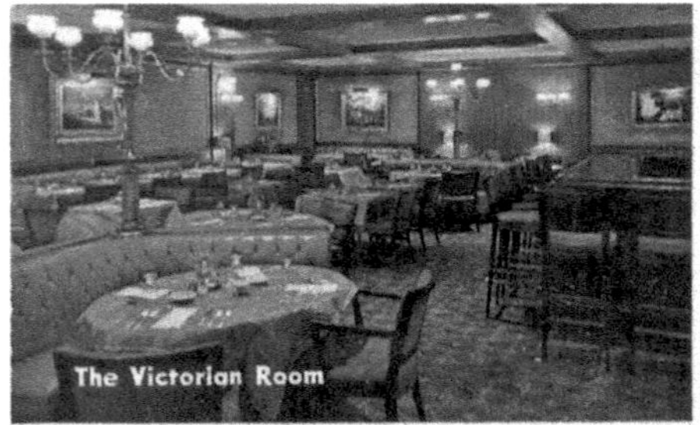

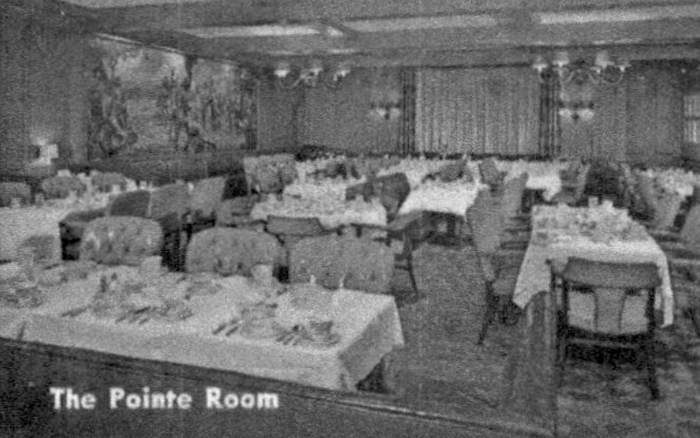

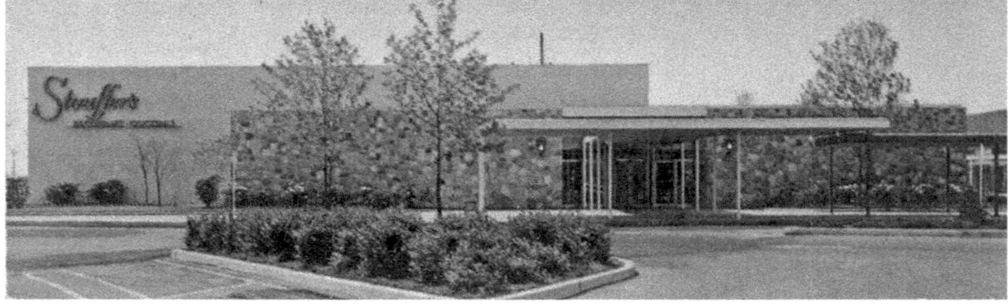

A multi-image postcard showing interior and exterior shots of the elegant Stouffer's Eastland location. *Author's collection.*

fieldstone exterior. The menu closely mirrored that of the downtown location and emphasized traditional American classics but with the creative twist for which Stouffer's was known: cheese soufflé with tomato sauce; creamed chicken and fresh mushrooms with toasted noodles; and roasted lamb sandwich gravy, French-fried potatoes and relish. Stouffer's well-burnished reputation as a quality choice for lunch in turn encouraged a robust dinner trade, which it also enjoyed for many years.

Part II

A Community of Many Colors: Ethnic Dining in Detroit

In an eclectic city like Detroit, the presence of various ethnic restaurants creates a quality that is ubiquitous yet strangely unacknowledged at the very same time. That quality is a *de facto* type of social integration—and the opportunity it provides for understanding cultures other than one's own. In yesteryear's Detroit, this was even truer than it is today. In Europe, the distance between a German biergarten and an Italian ristorante was hundreds of miles. In Detroit, it could have been just a few blocks.

Locating these eateries used to be fairly easy. During much of the twentieth century, boundaries between neighborhoods were more clearly defined than today. If you were looking for Polish golanka or Italian carbonara or maybe Irish black pudding, you'd know what part of town to head to. And oftentimes, a characteristic style of architecture would signal an eatery's identity, a trend that continues today. The familiar Alpine façade denotes a German restaurant. White stucco walls and the wavy, terra-cotta roofs indicates a Mexican cantina, and a square cupola paired with double-hung windows suggests an Italian ristorante.

What ethnic restaurants do best is offer diners an experience that is different from what they usually eat. In a 1985 review in the *Detroit Free Press*, writer Linda Solomon offered an interesting if slightly pessimistic insight: "One reason way fast food is so popular: there are no surprises. Big Macs from Warren taste the same as Big Macs sold in New Jersey. But try a mom and pop restaurant advertising home cooking, and it's a gamble."

Traditional ethnic restaurants are still around today, but permanently altered urban neighborhoods have given way to suburban sprawl, making them somewhat harder to find. But in one way this may be a plus for the spontaneous diner—taking a drive to an unfamiliar area can lead to an unexpected surprise.

Ethnic restaurants of yesteryear were often family-owned concerns that operated from a single location. Many failed to survive past their founders' generation but, ironically, were often responsible for creating the most indelible memories for their guests. This part pays them homage.

7

Arabic

The Sheik

It's probably no coincidence that The Sheik, perhaps one of the finest Arabic restaurants in the nation, was located just around the corner from Greektown, as Greek and Arabic food share many similarities.

But at the same time, The Sheik persistently maintained its individuality. Standing guard over the corner of East Lafayette Street and Randolph Avenue, this Detroit destination was founded in 1940 by Fadel "Fred" Ganem, an immigrant from Syria. The quarters were small and the atmosphere intimate—despite the foreboding presence of the Wayne County Morgue across the street.

A 1958 review in the *Detroit Times* states the dining at The Sheik "is the very best of old Araby." The food was what the discriminating fan of Syrian and Lebanese food would expect—hummus with tahini, a mixture of mashed chickpeas with sesame seed butter; kibbee, baked ground lamb wrapped in wheat bread; and a bevy of side dishes like squash or stuffed grape leaves. For many years, The Sheik was widely recognized as one of the finest Arab restaurants in the nation. Its intimate, homelike setting made it an especially good place for a couple on a date.

The Sheik was a durable downtown institution. Fadel ran his eatery until retiring in 1968, when he turned the reigns over to his son-in-law Ed Michael. After Ed passed away in the late 1970s, his widow, Esther, maintained the restaurant and purchased the building next door to add an additional dining room.

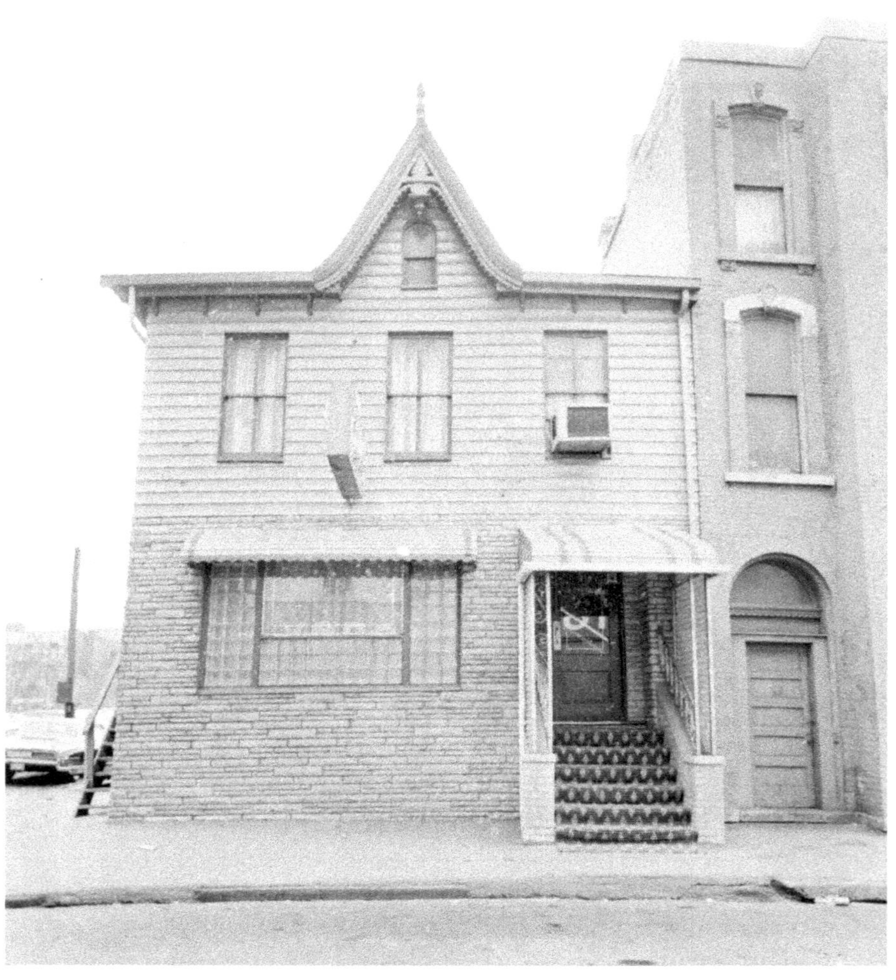

Taking the prize for anonymity, the Sheik occupied an obscure former house on East Lafayette Boulevard at Randolph Street. *Courtesy of the Walter Reuther Library.*

Ultimately, however, the crowds began to thin as the regular patrons began to either die off or move to the outer-ring suburbs. In 1990, The Sheik finally closed.

8

Chinese

Chin Tiki

Beginning in the late nineteenth century, Chinese Americans began to move eastward, usually to escape prejudice on the West Coast. Detroit's small Chinese community first settled just north of Michigan Avenue and the John Lodge Freeway, near where MGM Casino now stands. On the surrounding blocks, many of the newcomers established their own businesses, including numerous Chinese restaurants and laundries.

When Marvin Chin established his restaurant, the Chin Tiki, on Cass Avenue in 1967, his timing proved fortuitous. A 2009 article in the *Detroit Free Press* explained why: "Chin Tiki opened in 1967, near the end of America's postwar obsession with Polynesian culture that began with the Broadway musical (1949) and film version (1958) of 'South Pacific,' based on James Michener's 1948 novel 'Tales of the South Pacific.'"

The establishment rode this wave of popularity over the next several decades, attracting a wide cross section of locals and an occasional celebrity. Muhammad Ali and Joe DiMaggio were regulars. Chin Tiki successfully merged the restaurant and nightclub concept under one roof, and its heavy use of Polynesian décor fueled its popularity. The *Detroit Free Press* article continued: "The upscale dining establishment sported an ornately decorated downstairs lounge restaurant, complete with towering tiki statues, waterfalls and a bamboo bridge. An upstairs banquet facility was home to Hawaiian themed floor shows." A characteristically Polynesian menu complemented an array of rum-based libations.

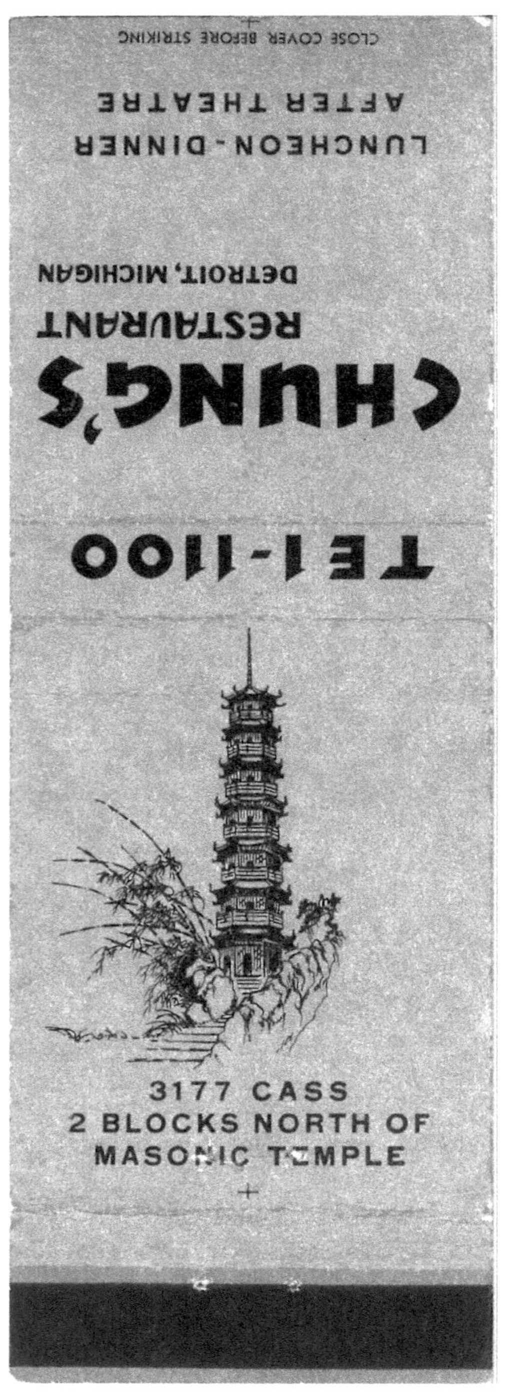

But like many popular downtown spots, changing demographics caused a steep decline in business at Chin Tiki, and in 1980, Marvin Chin decided to close the restaurant. The building briefly saw new life, however, in 2001, when a scene from the quintessential Detroit movie *8 Mile* was filmed inside. In the semibiographical film, rap singer Eminem's character, Jimmy, is seen singing "Chin Tiki Girls," one of the movie's several rap songs. After Chin died in 2006, the building was purchased by Olympia Development, which demolished it in 2009. Today, the site is included in the area slated for the District Detroit, the large sports and entertainment area built around Little Caesar's Arena, the new Detroit Red Wings hockey venue.

A vintage matchbook cover from the second location of Chung's, on Cass Avenue at Peterboro Street. *Author's collection.*

Chung's

By the mid-1950s, construction of the John Lodge Freeway had forced Chinatown to move from its original location near Michigan Avenue and Third Street to an area about a mile uptown near Cass Avenue and Peterboro Street. While many businesses failed to make the transition successfully, Chung's succeeded.

Chung's original location on Third Street was begun in 1940 by husband and wife Harry Chung and Shee Chin (whose brother Marvin Chin was the proprietor of Chin Tiki). After Harry's death in 1950, his wife continued to operate the restaurant, eventually moving it to the new Chinatown neighborhood. Throughout its long life, Chung's specialized in classic Cantonese dishes and offered a consistent menu featuring what restaurant critic Molly Abraham described as "the old war horses from chow mein, sweet and sour pork and almond bones chicken to breaded fried shrimp."

From its earliest years, the restaurant was recognized as a center of the community. Until his untimely death in 1950, Harry Chung enjoyed the status of being the unofficial mayor of the original Chinatown. His obituary in the *Detroit News* described other roles he fulfilled at his restaurant: "At the same address, he maintained his home and office, which early on became a clearing house for civic activities of his people. There Detroit Chinese came often with business problems and family troubles."

Shee Chung's son Philip and nephew Allen Chin continued to operate the restaurant, eventually opening a second location in Waterford in 1993. But back in Detroit, the urban ills of crime and prostitution made the Cass Avenue area (derisively referred to as the "Cass Corridor") increasingly inhospitable, while most Chinese residents had long since moved to the suburbs. In 2000, Chung's—which by then was one of the very last vestiges of Chinatown—closed but left a storehouse of treasured memories in the hearts of metro Detroit's Chinese community. But hope has indeed sprung eternal for the Cass Avenue building. In 2015, the area's growing popularity due to its proximity to Little Caesar's Arena, the new venue for the Detroit Red Wings, caught the eye of the Diamond Jim Brady's restaurant group. A longtime fixture on the local dining scene, Brady's announced its plans to purchase and rehab the structure for a new restaurant. At this writing, the new venue is expected to open in early 2017.

Mannia Café

Restaurants that were established during the mid-twentieth century were often located in free-standing buildings, and if a particular such structure was built from scratch, it often exemplified the Midcentury Modern style popular at the time. Historian Tim Samuelson has identified the building as an example of "Googie" architecture, which is "a term used for the fantasy whimsical architecture of old drive-in restaurants." Samuelson adds that "although definitely designed to be showy, the distinctive exterior walls are actually real structural forms shaped into an eye-catching presence."

Today, the hulk of the then trendy building is all that remains of Stanley Chung's Mannia Café, located at 265 East Baltimore Avenue—about two and one half blocks east of Woodward Avenue. But when the building was completed in 1968, it represented the dogged determination of Stanley and his brother Oscar to stick with and support the city of Detroit in the aftermath of the 1967 insurrection. During that disturbance, Oscar's restaurant, the Ten Sheng Ten on West Warren Avenue, was destroyed by a fire that spread from the building next door. He rebuilt at the same location and eventually sold the Ten Sheng Ten and joined Stanley in his new venture, located in the historic Milwaukee Junction neighborhood—the area where the city's very first automotive plants were located.

In 1968, Stanley opened his sleek new establishment, featuring upscale Chinese cuisine. A newspaper advertisement of the era promotes "exotic Chinese-American dining, where it is important that everything be exactly right." As the area's racial makeup changed, the restaurant changed with it, offering an occasional "Rhythm Kitchen" atmosphere, which featured artists performing reggae, jazz, ballroom classic and the new and emerging hip-hop genres of music.

Eventually Stanley opened another location, Stanley's Other Place at Woodward Avenue and Eight Mile Road.

The Baltimore Avenue restaurant enjoyed a run of almost thirty years before the usual culprits—crime and urban blight—reduced the flow of patrons to a mere trickle. But the building's unusual architecture proved fortuitous. After closing in 1995, the building served as a church for several years. Period photos suggest the building's unusual architecture presaged its second life.

9

French

Pontchartrain Wine Cellars

A quiet venue tucked behind its namesake hotel (but sharing no affiliation), the Pontchartrain Wine Cellars represented a gracious nod to the city's French heritage. After landing in July 1701, Antoine de la Mothe Cadillac originally named his new outpost Fort Pontchartrain du Détroit in honor of Louis Phélypeaux, Comte de Pontchartrain, Minister of Marine to King XIV of France. The modern-day restaurant was located on the very same spot.

The quaint, red brick nineteenth-century building century seemed an idyllic setting for a fine restaurant but was not the Wine Cellar's original home. In 1935, Hank Borgman opened the PWC at 618 Wayne Street (now Washington Boulevard), where it flourished for over twenty years. In 1956, Borgman's daughter moved the restaurant to its Larned Street location. Joe Beyer bought the business in 1971 and continued its legacy. He took pride in being very hands on, regularly greeting and occasionally seating his devoted patrons.

Here, the wine took center stage, featuring extensive offerings of European (especially French) and American inebriants. A 1936 display ad in the *Detroit Free Press* described the institution as a "Parisian Bistro" featuring a "Library of Wines." Local lore has it that Cold Duck was invented at the PWC in 1937, when then owner Hank Borgman revived an old German custom of combining sparkling burgundy with champagne. The new beverage was a hit and brought the restaurant international recognition.

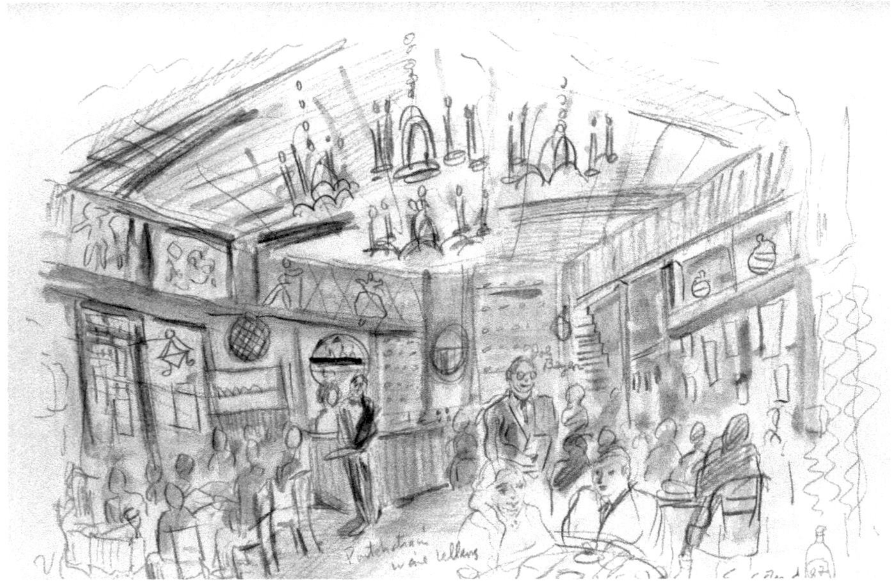

A whimsical drawing of the interior of the Pontchartrain Wine Cellars downtown on Larned Street. The gentleman in the center is owner Joe Beyer. Look closely to see his name just behind his image. *Courtesy of Charlie Langton.*

Menu items were consistently and unabashedly French, such as brochette of beef tenderloin and veal cordon bleu. For dessert, still hungry diners could choose between *pot de crème chocolat* or *petits babas au rhem* or *coconut bombe.* Diners probably didn't need to know French to appreciate these richly decadent *bonnes bouches*.

Besides attracting its regular devotees, the PWC was popular for couples enjoying a special night out or for a big-spending high school guy looking to impress his prom date. An anonymous blogger who identifies himself simply as the "Wine Raconteur" offers this reflection on visiting the bistro:

> *I remember going there and starting off with Escargot, which was not a common offering back in the day, followed by another curiosity back then a bowl of French Onion soup. I also had one of my favorite dishes of my youth, which is no longer in vogue, a plate of Frog Legs Provencal. I finished the meal with my introduction to Peach Melba and of course a glass of Cold Duck. I cannot remember what my date had, but I do remember that she was shocked that I was dining on frog legs, as that was a creature that one dissected in a Biology class in High School.*

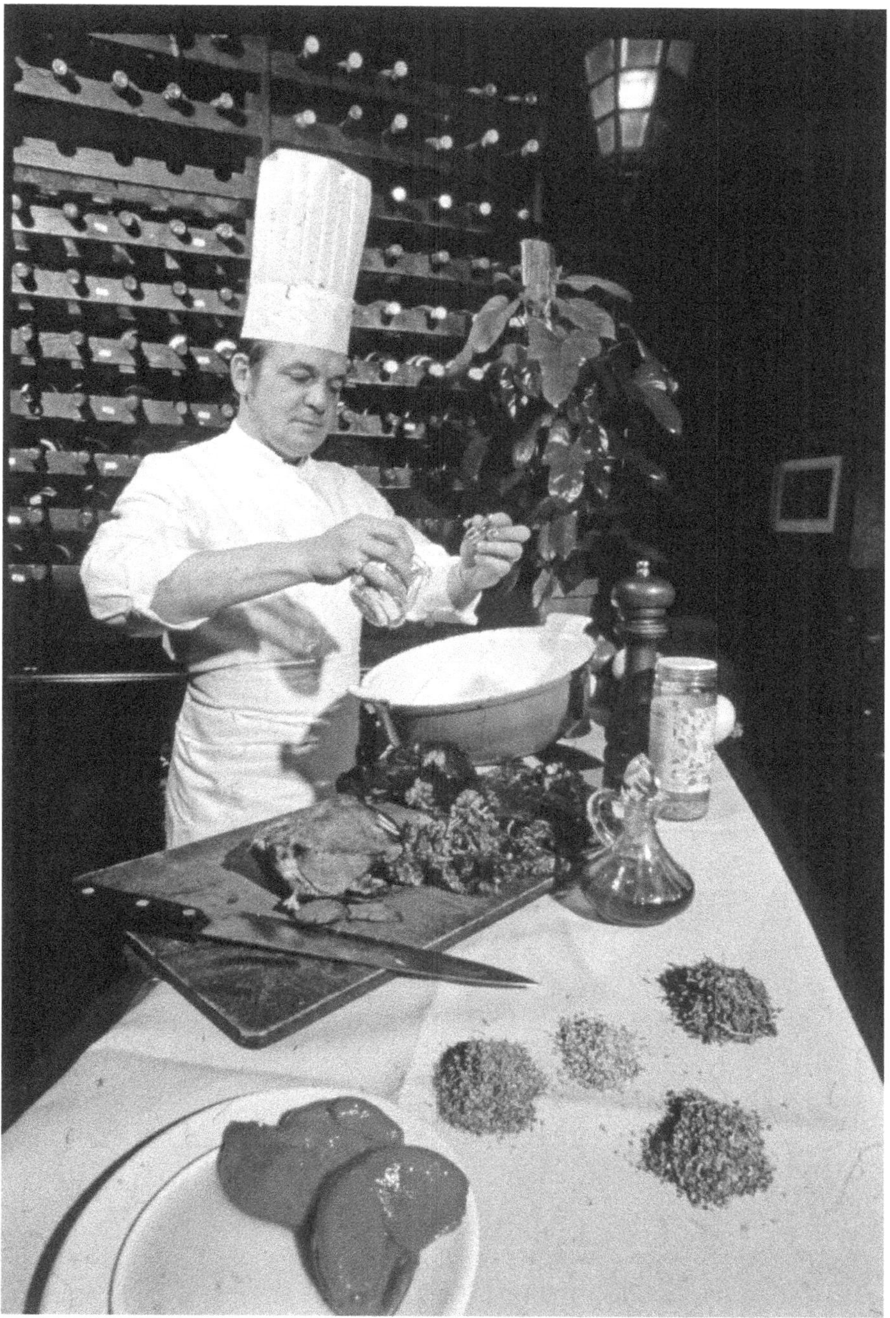

Chef Ray Schwartz performs a demonstration at the Pontchartrain Wine Cellars. *Courtesy of the Walter Reuther Library.*

Sadly, a convergence of several forces spelled doom for the restaurant beginning in the late 1980s. Changing consumer tastes, an aging clientele and disruption caused by construction at nearby Cobo Center all cut into its business. In 1991, after years of struggle, Beyer was forced to file for bankruptcy and close his quaint French bistro. Over the next few decades the elegant building housed a variety of tenants, including a Mexican restaurant—followed by years of abandonment.

But recently, it got a new lease on life. At this writing, the old headquarters of the Detroit Fire Department next door is being converted to the Foundation Hotel, a boutique establishment, to serve the Detroit's burgeoning convention trade. The two buildings share a common wall, and plans call for an archway to be created to make the vintage restaurant space an extension of the hotel lobby.

10

German

Dakota Inn Rathskeller

Ethnic restaurants are often fond of marketing their place by saying, "Once you walk in the door, you'll feel like you're in [insert name of foreign nation here]." Most places sincerely mean it, but no place in Detroit does it quite like the Dakota Inn Rathskeller.

In 1933, Karl Kurz, an enterprising emigrant from Bavaria, saw the growing German community in his east side neighborhood around Six Mile and John R. Sensing an opportunity with the repeal of Prohibition, Kurz decided to purchase what had been a Chinese laundry on John R. at West Dakota Street and transform it into an authentic rathskeller, a German word that refers to a bar or pub located in the cellar or basement of a town hall. Partially true to the term, the Dakota Inn actually has a separate drinking room in its basement.

Kurz decided to model his establishment after those in his hometown of Wiekersheim, Germany. One look around and you'll see just how meticulous his efforts were. Curved archways, dark oak paneling and deer heads on the wall create just the right atmosphere for enjoying truly authentic German dishes, including *kartoffelpuffer* (potato pancake served with applesauce), *schweinefleisch* (pork loin with potatoes and red kraut) or *schweinefleisch schnitzel* (sautéed pork cullet).

But the food is just the beginning. Equally essential to the Dakota Inn experience is the beer (dozens of varieties—both domestic and, of course,

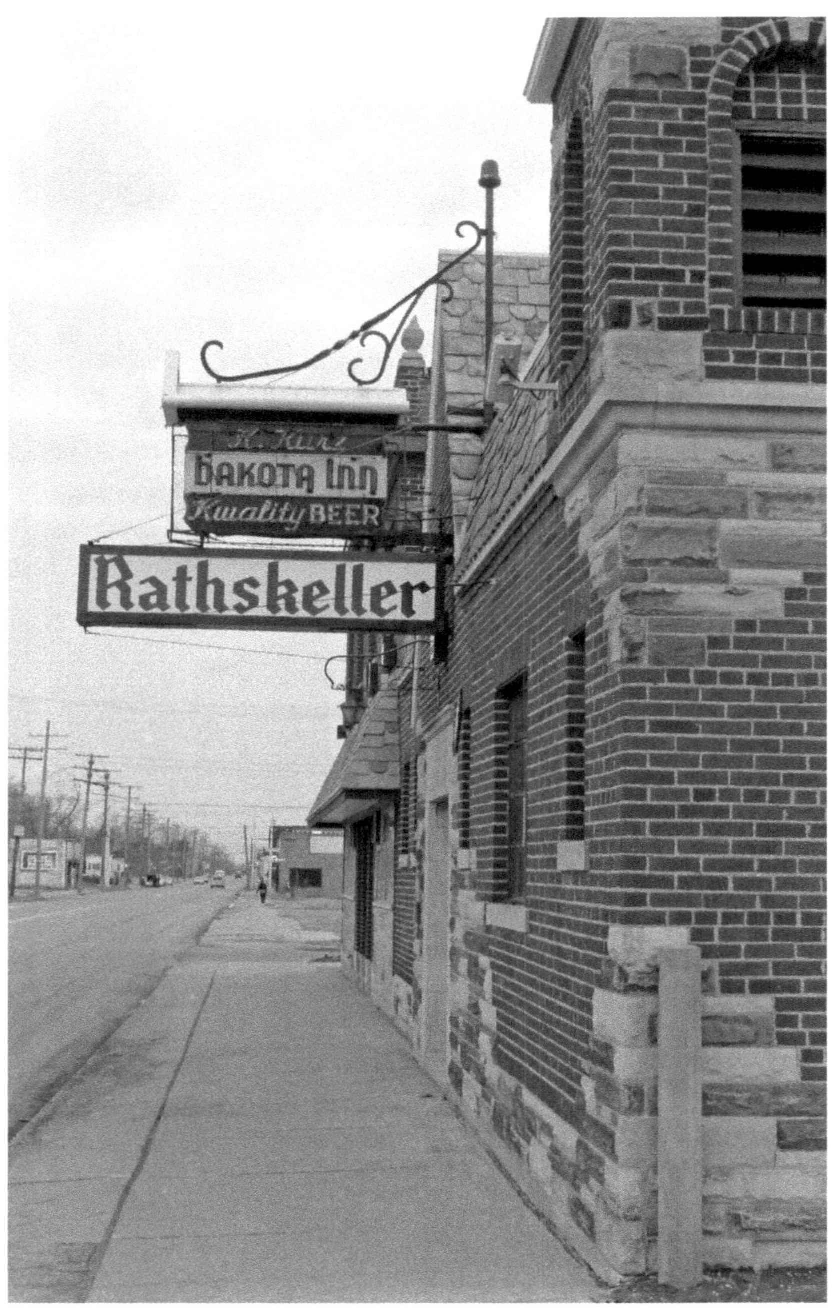

Karl Kurz spared no effort to make his Dakota Inn Rathskeller resemble an authentic German original as closely as possible. *Courtesy of the author.*

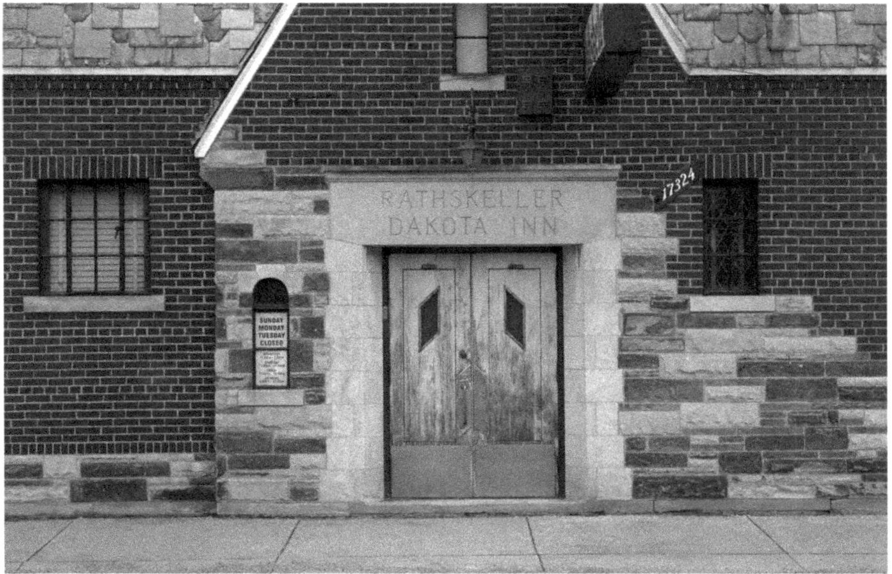

Despite its location in a rough neighborhood, the Dakota Inn remains a local favorite, attracting a robust crowd every Saturday night. *Courtesy of the author.*

German imports) and the raucous entertainment, which climaxes when the organist leads the crowd in the singalong around the *schnitzelbank*, a woodworker's bench. A longtime German tradition, Kurz etched the words on the wall: Question: *Ist Das Nicht'ne Schnitzelbank*? Answer: *Ja das Ist'ne Schnitzelbank.*

A 1983 article in the *Detroit Free Press* states that during World War II the words were covered with an American flag in deference to the Unites States' combat role.

But fortunately the *Schnitzelbank* reappeared once the hostilities ended. At the Dakota Inn today, it's a time-honored weekend ritual.

The Little Café

For most Americans, the more authentic an ethnic restaurant is, the more fascinating it becomes. For this reason, non-German patrons relished a visit to the Little Café on Gratiot Avenue and no doubt kept coming and coming—for over fifty years. Opened in 1935 by Frau Anna Born, the Bavarian-style restaurant in a heavily German neighborhood paid faithful

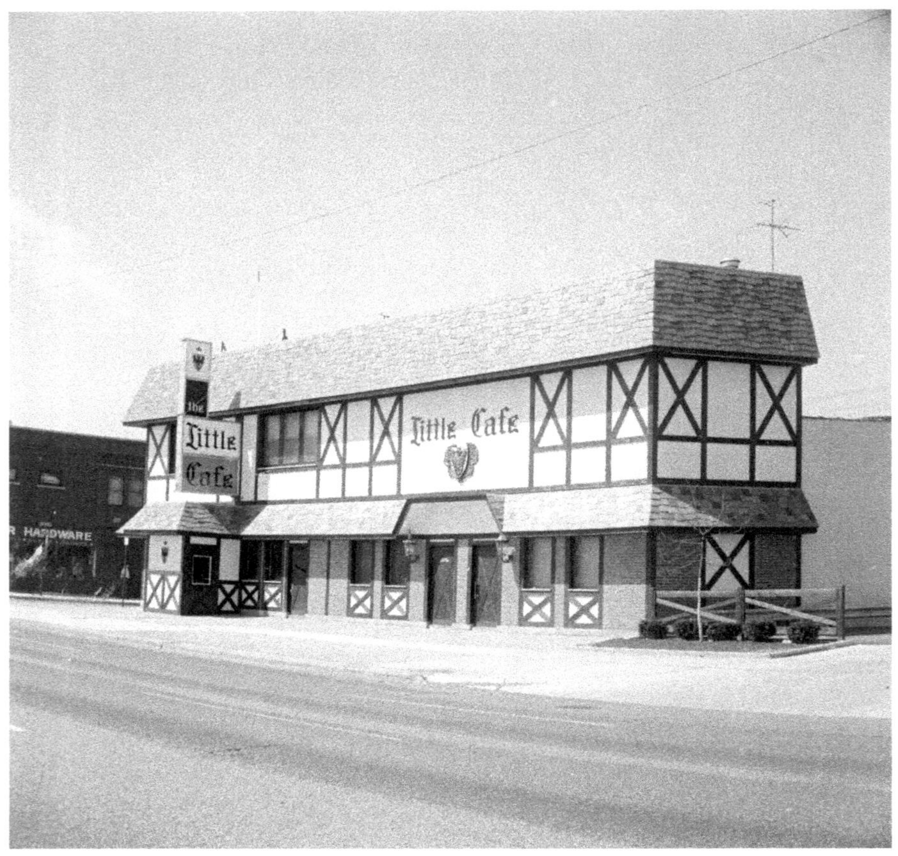

The ever popular Little Café on Gratiot Avenue. Most of the city's landmark German restaurants were located at various points on the city's east side. *Courtesy of the Walter Reuther Library.*

homage to the cuisine of its ancestral homeland, offering dishes like *hassenpfeffer* (rabbit marinated in wine gravy and roasted) and *kassler rippchen* (smoked pork) plus more familiar choices like sauerbraten and weiner schnitzel. A few American entrées rounded out the otherwise faithful German menu.

The combination of authenticity and high quality drew the accolades of critics. In a January 1964 review, the *AAA Motor News* offer these comments: "Diners here can choose from American or German foods which are ala carte weekdays, full dinners on weekends. Complete dinner meals are served with light drop noodle chicken soup, five portion salad tray (TV travel man George Pierrott has said the red cabbage here will make a vegetarian out of anyone), basket of rolls, dessert and coffee."

With a description like this, it's easy to imagine stepping in from a cold rainy Gratiot Avenue for a good hot German meal!

Besides a menu as authentic as anything this side of the Rhine, the Little Café was known for a wide selection of German beer—light and dark—on tap, as opposed to more common of practice today, where bottles of Beck's or Holsten Pilsener round out the offerings. There was one other unusual feature—a bowling alley. Originally connected to the restaurant via an archway, the facility was later moved upstairs to allow for more parking space.

The waitstaff at the Little Café was always the epitome of professionalism, specializing in offering a warm Germanic welcome.

Schweizer's

Modern cities tend to be highly segmented. Thanks largely to twentieth-century zoning, everything seems to be assigned its proper place—homes, retail shops and factories all occupy their appropriate niche.

But a few vestiges of an earlier era remain. Just east of the Renaissance Center, the blocks that straddle Woodbridge, Franklin and Riopelle Streets were once known as the warehouse district, where pre-1900 machine shops (which represented the very beginning of the nascent auto industry) abutted corner taverns and tiny grocery stores. At 260 Schweizer Place, originally known as Hastings Street, a classic German restaurant made the neighborhood home from 1862 until 1991. Its tenure of well over a century was enough time for three generations of the family to practice their craft with consistency and style. Godfrey Schweizer opened the restaurant during the early years of the Civil War and was succeeded by his son Charlie shortly after his return from World War I. In 1933, Charlie retired, and his son Stewart (who was born in an upstairs room in 1895) took over, eventually transferring the reins to his children Betty and Bob.

The restaurant originally served only German fare, including *sauerbraten*, potato pancakes, pig hocks with sauerkraut and boiled potato and *weinerschnitzel*. Schweizer's was also known for its extensive selection of German beers and wines. The menu broadened over time, expanding to include things like ribs, steaks and fish entrées, but always retained its core ethnic offerings. Adjusting to his changing clientele proved to be a good business strategy for Stewart Schweizer. In a 1972 interview marking the restaurants' 110th anniversary, he facetiously remarked, "We've got too many Irish coming in now!"

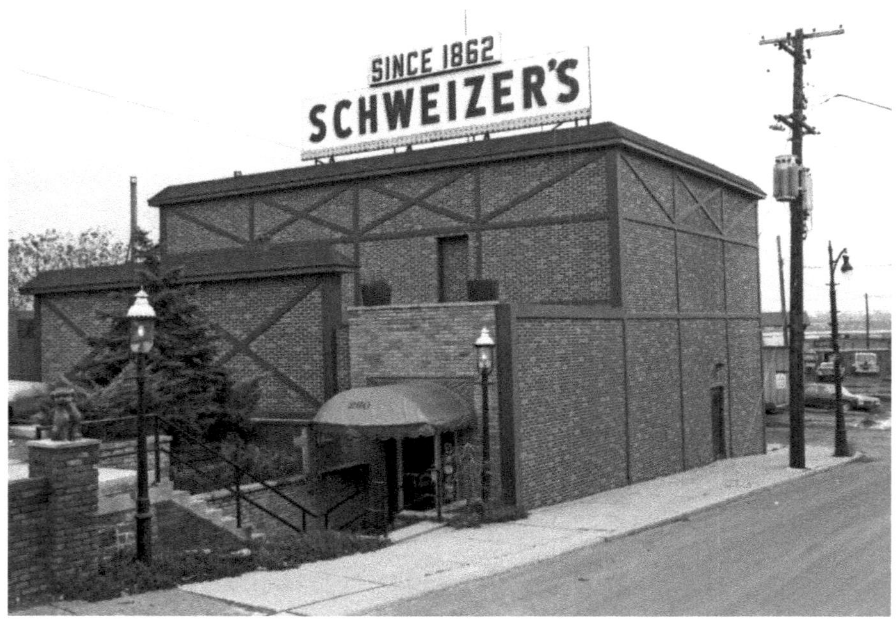

Exterior view of Schweizer's, an institution for authentic German dining for well over a century. Until its closing in 1991, it was Detroit's oldest restaurant. *Courtesy of the Walter Reuther Library.*

After a remarkable run of 129 years, Schweizer's ultimately closed in 1991. Another restaurant, Vondie's on the River, occupied the building for a short time. In recent years, a large swath of property in the area (including Schweizer's) was purchased by Riverfront Holdings, a real estate subsidiary of General Motors Company. In December 2014, the old restaurant and several neighboring buildings were demolished. The hope in the neighborhood is that positive redevelopment will replace the temporary sea of parking lots. But in recognition of the site's history, the street is still officially named Schweizer Place.

11

Greek

Grecian Gardens

In recent years, local commentators have lamented about the "de-Greeking" of Greektown, the much-loved area on the eastside of downtown traditionally known as Detroit's center of Greek culture. Today, while some semblance of the Greek atmosphere remains, much of neighborhood is dominated by chain hamburger joints and new, modern office buildings.

Decades ago, the milieu was markedly different. Clustered around the block of Monroe Street between Beaubien and St. Antoine Streets there were Hellenic grocery stores, coffeehouses, bakeries and restaurants. One such eatery was the legendary (or notorious, depending on your view) Grecian Gardens.

For the public, the taverna (as Greek restaurants were known), a relatively small dining room wedged in the center of the block, served a classic Greek American menu with items like *melitzanosalata* (eggplant dip) and *tirokafteri* (whipped feta cheese with hot peppers and olive oil dip), often served with *tzatziki* sauce (yogurt-garlic-cucumber dip), and Greek-influenced pasta dishes, such as *spaghetti Napolitano* and *pastitsio* (baked layers of thick pasta and minced meat mixture topped with a thick béchamel sauce).

To those with inside knowledge, however, owner Gus Colacasides was informally known as "the kingpin of Greektown." Frequent rumors of illegal gambling surrounded both Colacasides and his restaurant, which were given credence following a 1962 incident involving several Detroit

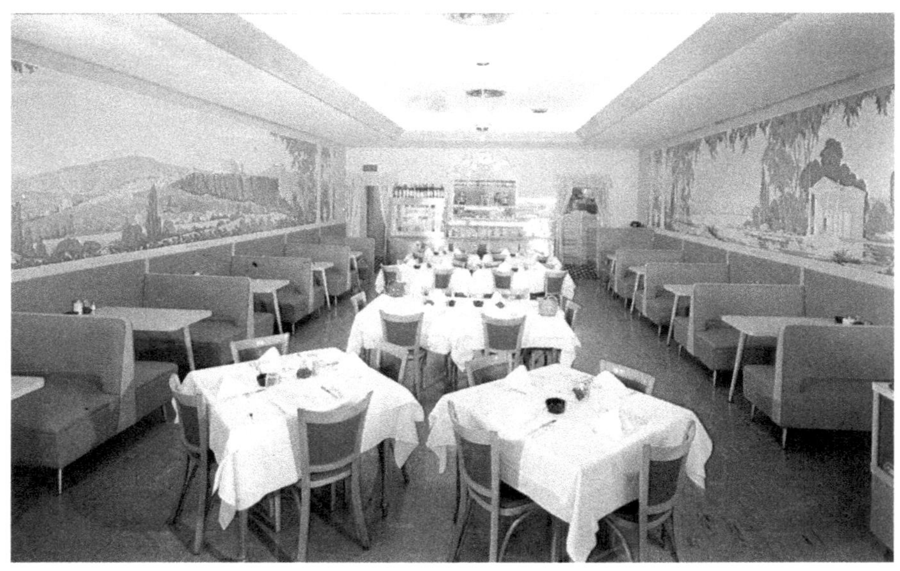

A postcard view of the storied dining room at the Grecian Gardens on Monroe Street. If only walls could talk! *Author's collection.*

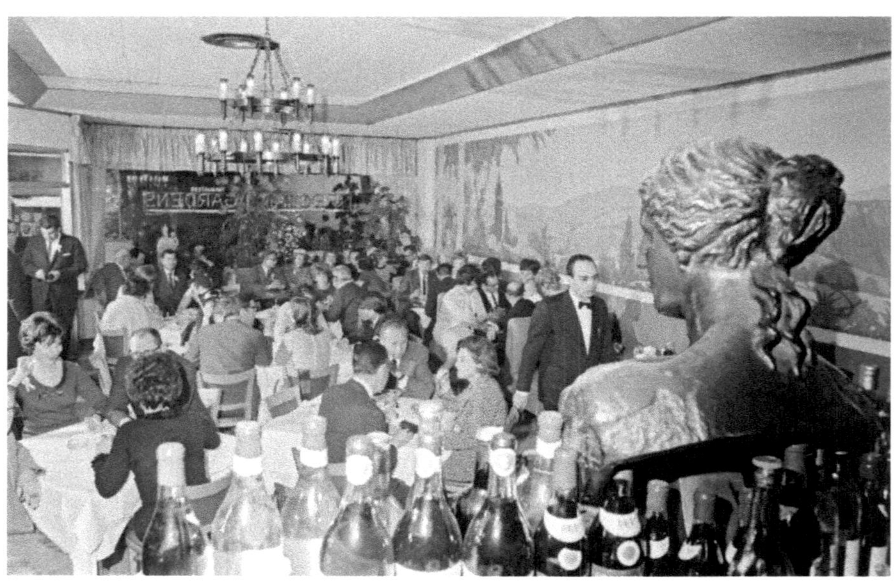

A vintage 1960s shot of the Grecian Gardens on a busy night. Like many Greektown establishments, the Grecian Gardens was popular in the non-Greek community. *Courtesy of the Walter Reuther Library.*

Lions players and the "Party Bus," a mob-run mobile venue used for illegal gambling, drinking and quite possibly prostitution. In his book, *Once in a Great City*, author David Maraniss described the backdrop, which intimately involved the restaurant:

> *The link between the Party Bus and the football players began in the drowsy early Saturday morning darkness of the previous August 18, when officers of the Criminal Investigation Bureau entered another hangout, the Grecian Gardens on Monroe Street in Greektown, only one block south of police headquarters. Inside they happened to see Wayne Walker, a Lions linebacker, sitting with the Giacalone brothers at a table in the back. Also visible was Jimmy Butsicaris, Alex Karras's pal who had brought him into part ownership of the Lindell Cocktail Bar. The officers had entered the restaurant based on a complaint of illegal liquor sales, but now they had something more to interest them, so they left and staked out the scene from their car. The Grecian Gardens, as it happened was a familiar Lions' lair, much like the Lindell. The players often had what they called Loyalty Parties there, a night of male bonding, team building and prodigious drinking without management, coaches or wives. But this was not the cleanest crowd for Walker to be seen with, not with Tony Jack and Billy Jack at the table, and so many other underworld characters connected to the place. The bar operator, Gus Colacasides, considered the kingpin of Greektown gambling, kept secret black books of gamblers and bribable lawmen. The building was owned by the widow of the late Pete Corrado, known as "The Enforcer" during his heyday in the rum-running Prohibition era, when the Detroit River, with Canadian booze on the other side, swarmed with smugglers. Two modern day enforcers, Sammy Giordano and Pete Vitale, worked at the Gardens now, and a Corrado son, Anthony, provided muscle for the Giacalones.*

What followed was an investigation of the Detroit Lions organization, a number of police officers and several individual players by the Detroit Police Department and the National Football League, ultimately resulting in fines and suspensions for members of each group.

HELLA'S CAFÉ

Maybe it was due to its prime corner location or to its larger-than-life owner, but most longtime frequenters of Greektown will generally agree that Hella's Café at Monroe and St. Antoine Streets was perhaps the most durable fixture on the block.

Opened in 1901, Hella's was considerably larger than many of its competitors and sported an interior accentuated by dark wood and dim lighting. At some point in the restaurant's history, Gus Anton, son of the owner, took over managing the business. Gus had a very "hands on"

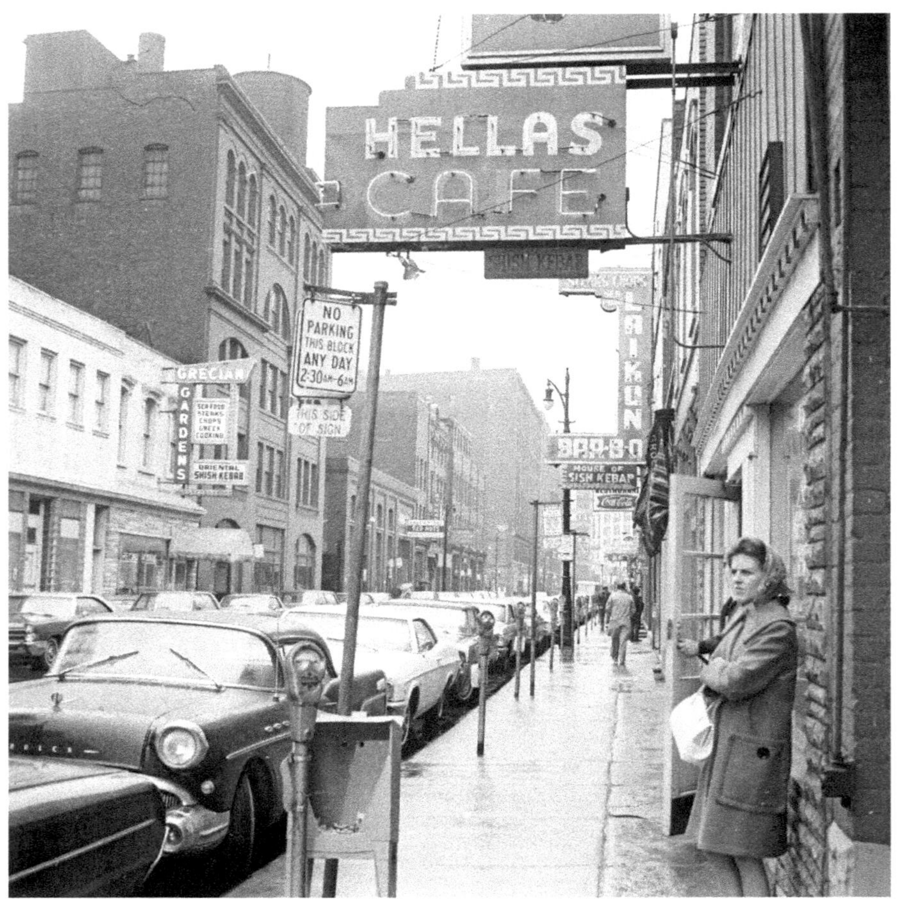

A 1966 view of Monroe Street on a rainy day, with Hella's in the foreground. Note the period signs of the block's competing eateries. *Courtesy of the Walter Reuther Library.*

approach, often greeting patrons at the door and even waiting on tables. Multiple visitors to the blog Tour De Hood speak fondly of Hella's as the place they often began an evening during their youth.

Hella's was known for its first-rate Greek cuisine but was especially renowned for super tender lamb shanks and saganaki, or "flaming cheese," that, when lit, seemed to produce a higher flame than the other restaurants in Greektown—maybe due to the higher ceiling! Local legend has it that Gus brought the saganaki gimmick to Detroit in the 1970s after seeing it at a Greek restaurant in Chicago.

In 2008, Gus, who had reached the age of eighty and lacked an heir, decided to close his restaurant after a 107-year run. "I'm very sad, naturally," Gus said at the time. "But at my age, what can you do? I'm old. I need the rest."

A few years later Gus licensed the Hella's name to investors working to re-create the concept in Farmington Hills. Despite opening to rave reviews in 2013, the new, larger Hella's could not duplicate the magic of the downtown original. Within a couple years, the revived concept failed.

Gus did eventually sell the downtown building, and for a time, rumors circulated that it would be converted to an Italian restaurant. Unfortunately, the plans did not materialize, and the building was eventually razed. Today, a vacant lot—highly unusual for the neighborhood—sticks out like a real sore thumb.

12

Italian

Lelli's Inn

Prince Clemens von Metternich, a European diplomat during the nineteenth century, was famous for saying, "Italy is not a country, it's a geographical expression." When it comes to dissecting the differences between regional Italian cuisines, his analogy seems spot on. Where southern Italian food tends to feature pastas and tomato-based sauces, its northern counterpart reflects the characteristics of its neighbors: France, Switzerland and Austria—beef, polenta, beans and a few egg-based pastas with cream and butter.

Italian restaurants in Detroit have generally hewed closer to the northern traditions. Perhaps the grande dame was Lelli's Inn, located on Woodward Avenue at Bethune Street just north of the New Center neighborhood. Visiting the Lelli's was not just a dining experience, but also an education in how old Detroit "supper clubs" once operated. Waiters—older, male, tuxedoed and mostly Italian—seemed to glide effortlessly through series of dining rooms, never obtrusive but always accessible. Meals were proportioned to the *very* hearty appetite—consisting of a relish tray, salad, soup, pasta, the main course and, if the patron was willing to stretch his stomach still further, dessert, such as tiramisu, crème brulée or spumoni ice cream. A number of dishes were partially prepared tableside, including chateaubriand for two or a porterhouse steak carved for four.

Consistently busy at both lunch and dinner, Lelli's appeal extended throughout southeast Michigan and became known as a great place to dine before a show at the Fisher Theatre or a Detroit Symphony concert at Orchestra Hall.

Founded by Nerio and Irene Lelli in 1939, the restaurant was actually an old, retrofitted house abutting a former warehouse that was used for valet parking. Makeshift additions and renovations were done sporadically over the decades, which only seemed to add to the charm of the old place. Sadly, in 2000, the storied eatery succumbed to a fire, ending a long-standing tradition. The Lellis' descendants have revived the concept at two Oakland County locations, but neither can quite match the chemistry of the original.

Larco's Inn

Related to the Lelli family (see previous section), the Larcos presented a similar dining experience to that offered by their cousins but on a slightly smaller scale. Located between the campuses of Marygrove College and the University of Detroit, the welcoming bistro was popular with students, faculty and administrators from both institutions, as well as a faithful group of west side regulars.

While the menu and serving style (multiple courses leading up to a main entrée of veal, beef or pasta) was virtually identical to Lelli's, Larco's had an alternative for the diner with a modest appetite. Called a "set up," the patron would be

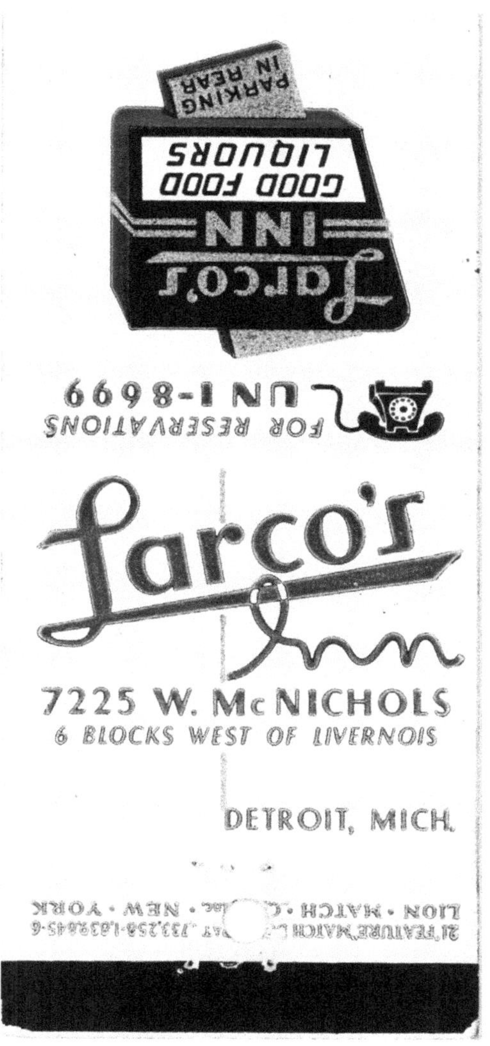

A vintage matchbook cover from the original Larco's location at 7225 McNichols Road. *Author's collection.*

served four small courses—antipasto tray, salad, soup and pasta. Basically, this included everything but the heavier main course. As customers became more health conscious, this option gradually became more popular.

But for those who had the stomach capacity for the set up *and* the main course, there was a tempting variety from which to choose; veal Colombo, veal Siciliano, the legendary filet mignon with zip sauce and chicken marsala, to name only a few.

Despite their similarity, the two restaurants each had its own core of loyal followers—both insisting that their establishment had the better minestrone or the tenderest filet. In reality, the families shared a close association—and probably the recipes as well.

But as the west side neighborhood declined through the 1970s and 1980s, the Larcos saw a drop off in their business. A devastating fire struck in 1985, and the family decided against rebuilding. Over the years, Larco's opened several suburban locations, but none had the staying power of the original. Today, the Larco name is relegated to Detroit dining history.

PARADISO CAFÉ

Driving north on Woodward Avenue approaching Six Mile Road, it was impossible to miss. A large rectangular blue sign emblazoned with an abstract curvy figure that vaguely resembled a whale. At night, its flashing lights highlighted the name—Paradiso—in white and red and competed with nearby buildings.

But despite the razzmatazz on the outside, inside the Paradiso was a simple, unassuming, yet consistently good Italian eatery. A 1978 review in the *Detroit Free Press* illustrated why the Paradiso was middle-class rather than high-end Italian. "The pasta department is run like a ladies' ready to wear counter: they invite you to mix and match. There are six pastas, spaghetti, vermicelli, fettucine, ravioli, mostaccioli and tortellini, and you can pick any one of those and then match it with any one of ten sauces."

Some of those sauces reflected the kitchen's creativity, which would send purists running for the door. One was a chef's special with creamed tuna and mushrooms. Other menu items included eggplant parmesan and a minestrone soup thicker and beefier than its competitors.

Whatever the restaurant's secret was, it certainly worked. The community eatery enjoyed a run of over forty years serving Detroit's less fussy

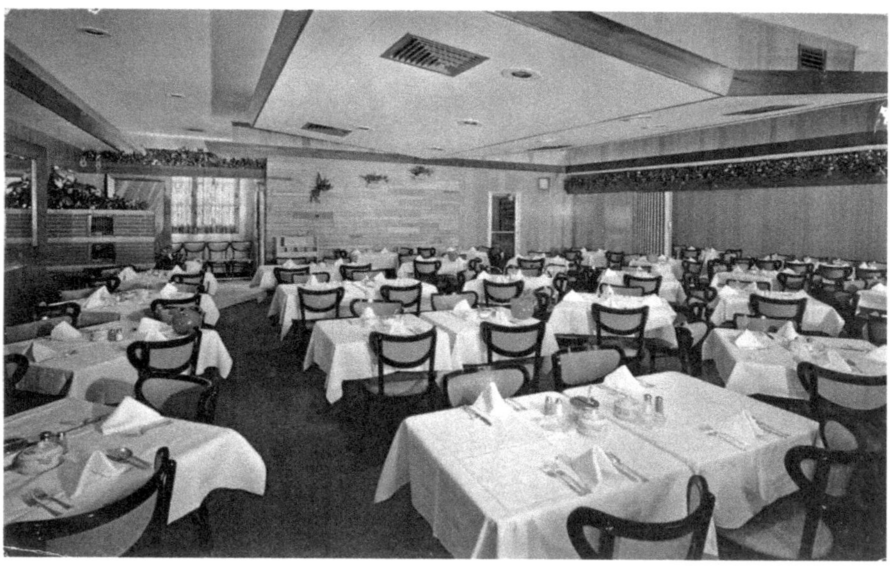

The dining room of the Paradiso Café on Woodward Avenue. It was a popular place in the 1950s and 1960s. *Author's collection.*

crowd. By the early 1980s, most of the Paradiso's regulars had migrated to the suburbs, eventually forcing it to close. The building saw a second life, however, when it was transformed into the Backstage, a Broadway-themed bar, restaurant and dinner theater.

Other places undoubtedly did Italian cuisine to a higher standard, but the atmosphere at the Paradiso harbored a special kind of feeling. The waitstaff, for example, was known to be overly friendly, even chummy, which may have been a clever marketing technique. A typical comment might be "Eat the [insert menu item here], honey. It's the best in town!"

ROMA CAFÉ

Restaurants that are links to bygone eras are always special. The more distant the founding date, the greater the fascination. The venerable Roma Café at 3401 Riopelle Street may not have quite the seniority of its counterparts in New York or Boston, but by Detroit standards, it's old—really old. In 1888, the Marazza family opened a rooming house at the corner of Russell and Riopelle Streets to accommodate traveling farmers

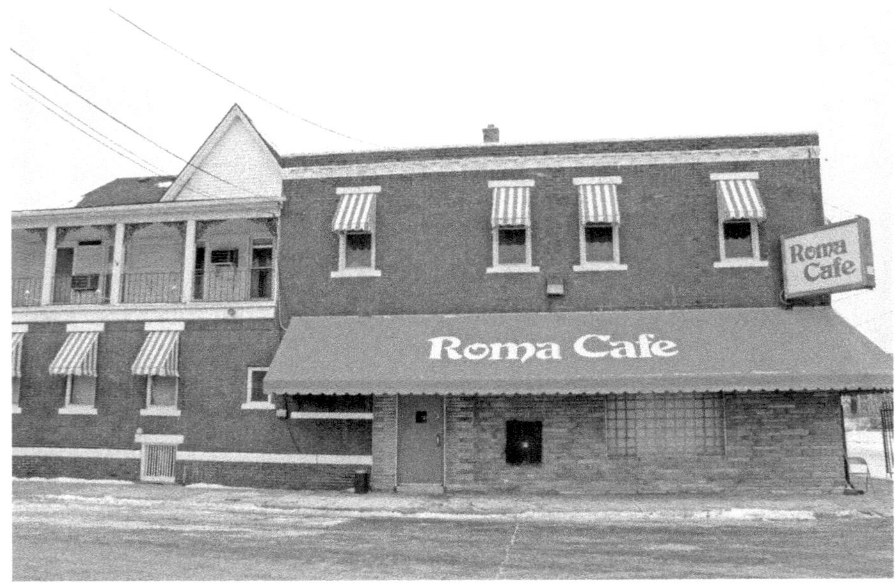

Exterior of the Roma Café, Detroit's oldest operating restaurant. *Courtesy of the author, with thanks to Janet Sossi Belcoure.*

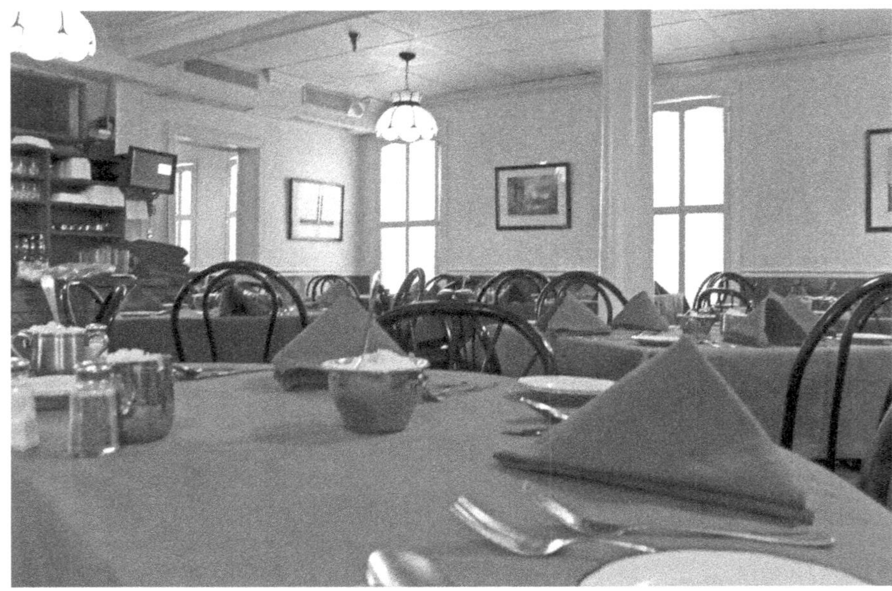

One of Roma Café's dining rooms. This storied restaurant has been serving generations of Detroiters the finest in Italian cuisine since 1890. *Courtesy of the author, with thanks to Janet Sossi Belcoure.*

who brought their produce to nearby Eastern Market. Standard practice at the time was for a meal to be included in the price of the lodging, hence the phrase "room and board"—the latter being a reference to a dining table. The sad reality, however, was that most such meals were of inferior quality, which provided Mrs. Marazza, a skilled Italian cook, with an opportunity. Soon she began to offer her superior home-cooked Italian meals to the guests at her home, resulting in loyalty that generated regular repeat business. A general store was soon added, offering customers common necessities of the day, including saddles and horse blankets. Eventually, the store was retired, and a café opened in its place.

In the early twentieth century, Morris Sossi, an executive with Fiat Motor Company of Italy, frequently found himself in Detroit while traveling for business. Frustrated by his inability to find quality Italian food, he eventually resorted to cooking his own meals on a hot plate in his hotel room. After receiving a suggestion to try Roma Café, Mr. Sossi instantly became a fan of the outstanding cuisine and close friends with the Marazzas, dining there every evening while in town.

By 1918, the Marazzas, wanting to retire and return to Italy, sold the restaurant to Mr. Sossi and a close friend, John Battaglia. At the same time, Mr. Sossi, who was not a chef by trade, sent for his brother and brother-in-law to emigrate from Italy to cook at the family's new restaurant. Just one year later, Mr. Battaglia met an untimely death, making the Sossis exclusive owners. The legendary bistro has remained in the family ever since. In 1940, Sossi's nephew Hector joined the staff, only to soon be drafted into the military. Returning after the end of World War II, Hector resumed working at the restaurant. Over the subsequent decades, he eventually became manager and ultimately the owner in 1965. In 1946, he met and fell in love with a young bookkeeper at the café, Stella, marrying soon after. Today, their spirited daughter, Janet Sossi Belcoure, runs the restaurant.

The story, however, has a curious parallel, as the Roma Café is not the family's only link to the food business. In 2012, *Michigan Restaurateur* magazine related a little-known story about Eugenio Sossi, Morris's brother and Janet's grandfather:

> *What's in a Name? Janet Sossi Belcoure's ties to chefs and the restaurant industry run deep. Her grandfather, Eugenio Sossi, was a European trained chef and traveled the United States opening kitchens at Statler-Hilton hotels. When it was time to open the kitchen at the Statler-Hilton in Cleveland, Ohio, Eugenio brought in his friend Ettore ("Hector"), a chef from Italy, to help.*

Eugenio and Ettore were close friends, so close that Eugenio named his son (Belcoure's father) "Hector" after his friend and fellow Italian chef. Around 1919, the job in Cleveland was finished, and Eugenio planned to move onto a Statler-Hilton in Buffalo, N.Y. Ettore, however, liked Cleveland and wanted to stay. Before parting, Ettore had a business proposition. He had an idea for putting spaghetti in a can, and asked Eugenio for $1,000 to help fund the startup. Eugenio thought the idea was crazy and, despite his love for his friend, declined the offer. That chef's last name was Boiardi, better known to American consumers as Chef Boyardee.

The food at Roma Café is as close to native northern Italian as one can imagine, owing no doubt to the Sossi family's passion for authenticity. Veal *scaloppine* marsala, chicken *scaloppine a la tosca* and breast of turkey *parmisiana* make customers know that they can order the real deal at the Roma—and generations of Detroiters have.

But Roma Café's influence does not stop at the city's borders. Scores of professional athletes, businesspeople and entertainers have made a visit a must when in Detroit. On one famous occasion in the late 1980s, Frank Sinatra, Liza Minelli and Sammy Davis Jr. stopped by unannounced on a late evening after performing at the Fox Theatre. The staff was about to close up, but the unexpected arrival prompted the night manager to phone Janet Sossi Belcoure, who had just arrived home. She instructed the staff to reopen for the famous trio. Belcoure herself returned, and the impromptu party lasted to 3:00 a.m. "Sammy went into the kitchen and thanked everyone for staying late, and the next night they sent their limousine driver over to pick up pasta and meatballs to enjoy backstage," said Belcoure.

Now that's Italian!

VANELLI'S

The Vanelli brothers typified the American dream. According to a 1959 review in the *Detroit Times*, Sam said that after arriving from Italy in the mid-1920s, he and his wife, Alba, soon began "kind of a boarding house and club at Mack and Gratiot Avenues where a few friends could drop by around for a glass of wine." Sam was obviously skilled with his euphemisms—"club" really meant "speakeasy"—but life under the Volstead Act might excuse his ambiguity. After Prohibition's repeal, Sam and his brothers converted the establishment into a legitimate bar and restaurant. Eventually, they relocated downtown to the Book Building on Washington Boulevard, before landing on Woodward in 1948.

By the postwar period, north Woodward (the stretch between Six and Eight Mile Roads) began to emerge as a sort of "restaurant row"—catering to newly affluent Detroiters. Vanelli's was a great example of this. The Vanelli brothers Sam, Al and Joe built their bistro in 1948 at 18300 Woodward Avenue, just north of Six Mile Road. Vanelli's represented a new, contemporary-style type of restaurant, more spacious and welcoming than many of its predecessors.

The Vanellis worked hard to reflect both their Italian heritage and their new American home in their menu. The offerings were basically composed of classics echoing the traditions of both Italy and the United States: chicken scaloppini, fettucine and mostaccioli, Dover sole, black sea bass and assorted ribs, steaks and chops.

One Italian tradition cherished at Vanelli's involved dessert. A display ad in a December 1951 edition of the *Detroit Free Press* encouraged regulars to bring their guests from out of town in for a holiday meal to be topped off by Dexter Daily Spumoni Ice Cream!

13

Jewish

Boesky's Deli

By the 1930s, the neighborhoods straddling west side streets like Dexter and Linwood Avenues and Twelfth Street were the center of Detroit's Jewish community. Densely packed with synagogues, kosher butchers and an array of secular businesses, the area teemed with pedestrians who flocked to the dozens of local restaurants, delis and supper clubs.

Early on, Boesky's emerged as a strong favorite. Run by the deli's eponymous clan of brothers, Abe, Bill, Harry, Sam and Sol, the business was originally located on the lower east side at Hastings and Farnsworth Streets. The move to Twelfth and Hazelwood Streets reflected the migration of the Jewish community and would become the cornerstone of a network of west side establishments that would include Darby's, Hazelwood Street and a second Boesky's on James Couzens Highway near Greenfield Road—with different family members manning the various outposts.

While the brothers no doubt wanted to appeal to a mixed clientele, their menu's mainstay was classic deli, especially popular in the Jewish community: pastrami, corned beef, chopped liver plus cheese blintzes and gefilte fish. Rounding it all out were steaks and chicken dishes.

But occasionally a restaurant's notoriety can come from an unexpected source. Such was the case at the Twelfth Street and Hazelwood location in the fall of 1937.

Boesky's, due to its notoriety, attracted a wide swath of humanity—including the much-feared Purple Gang, a notorious group of Jewish

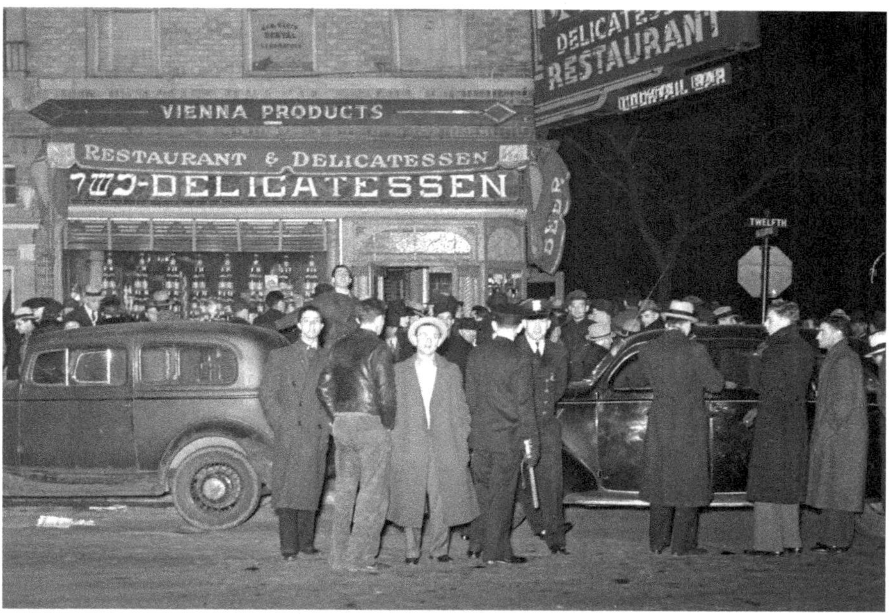

A crowd lingers in the middle of Twelfth Street after hired hitmen from New York murdered Harry Millman. *Courtesy of the Walter Reuther Library.*

mobsters. Organized crime in Detroit flourished during the 1920s and early 1930s due to Prohibition—and the proximity of Canada as a source of booze. The Purples and other Detroit syndicates made several fortunes until the amendment was repealed in 1933.

Organized crime had plenty of other business opportunities, however, including gambling, prostitution and selling "protection" to merchants. Lessons learned during Prohibition (i.e., respecting other groups' turfs) were not forgotten among members of the Purple Gang—with the notable exception of Harry Millman. Millman harbored an intense hatred for the Italians and made frequent attempts to muscle into their illegal numbers racket. Eventually, he got on the nerves of Italian mob's two top figures: Joe "Scarface" Bommorito and his brother-in-law Pete Licavoli. After obtaining preapproval from the Purple's boss Abe Bernstein, the Italians made several failed attempts to murder Millman, including planting a bomb under his car that instead killed his valet. Frustrated, they eventually hired two hitmen from New York. After stalking Millman for a few days and discovering his favorite hangouts, they located him standing alone at Boesky's bar during the early morning of November 25, 1937. The duo moved in and proceeded to unload their guns.

14

Mexican

Mexican Village

In the case of many ethnic restaurants, the business is often an extension of the family. And with some, an enlightened owner will treat everyone—employees and customers—with the same thoughtfulness and consideration she would afford to her own family.

Customers dining at Mexican Village pick this up right away—from the bowl of hot tortilla chips served as soon as you sit down to the speedy delivery of your food. Today, the family-dominated management insists that it remains that way.

In 1956, Fernando Gutierrez bought what was then a small cantina at Bagley Avenue and Eighteenth Street. At the time, ethnic restaurants catered to a much more insular clientele. Most of the patrons were themselves Mexican, many of them immigrants. The menu reflected that reality and consisted of items prepared exactly as they were in Mexico: beef tongue, brain tacos, et cetera. Fernando and his sister and partner Connie Bacigalupo promptly changed the offerings to appeal to a wider audience to include chimichangas, seafood enchiladas and fajitas tejanas.

Over the years the fledgling restaurant steadily thrived and expanded, gradually taking over some of the nearby shops to add additional dining space and a beautiful banquet room on the second floor. Lacking any formal training in business or restaurant operations—her only experience was working in her father's tortilla factory as a youngster—Connie explained she "basically just learned the trade by doing it."

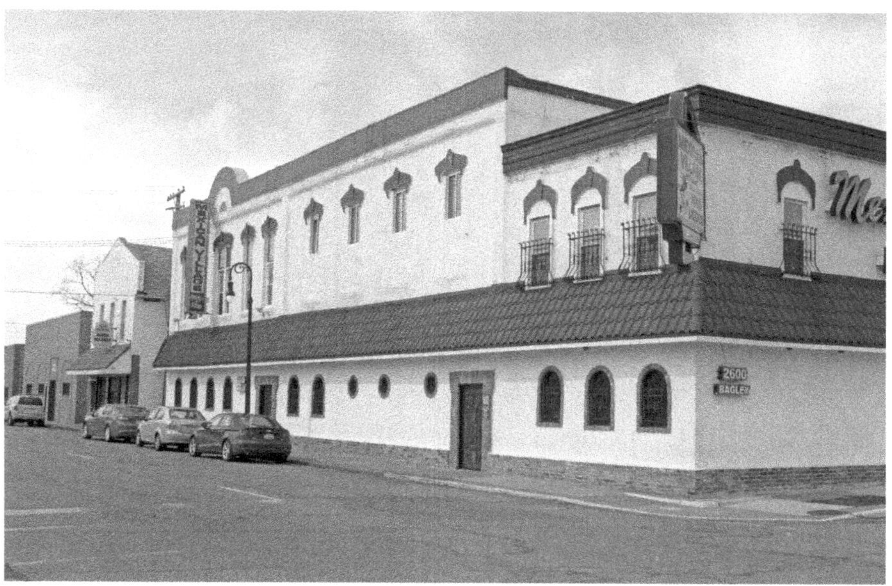

Originally just a small café (the portion on the right of the image), Mexican Village has grown over the years, taking up half a city block. *Courtesy of the author, with thanks to Connie Bacigalupo.*

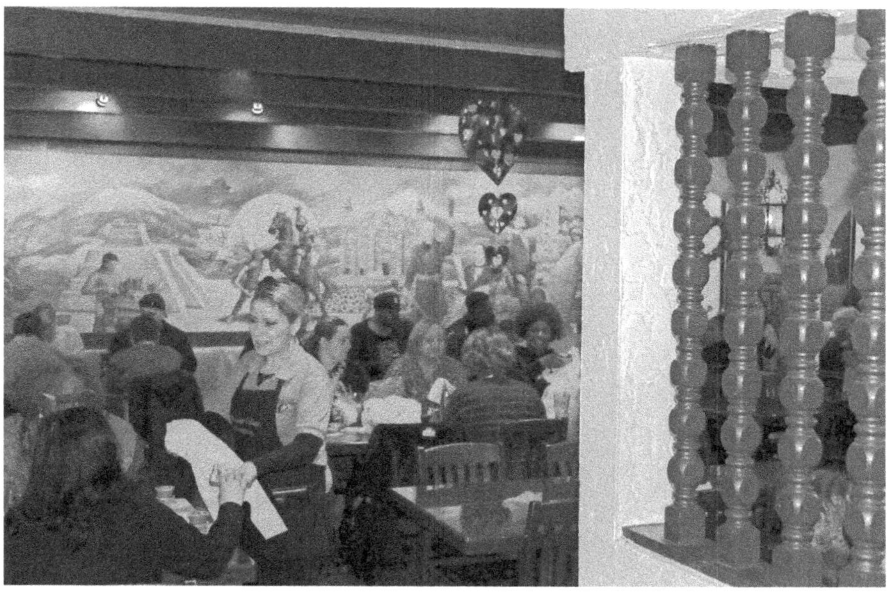

Picturesque murals adorn the walls of Mexican Village, the premier cantina of Mexicantown. *Courtesy of the author, with thanks to Connie Bacigalupo.*

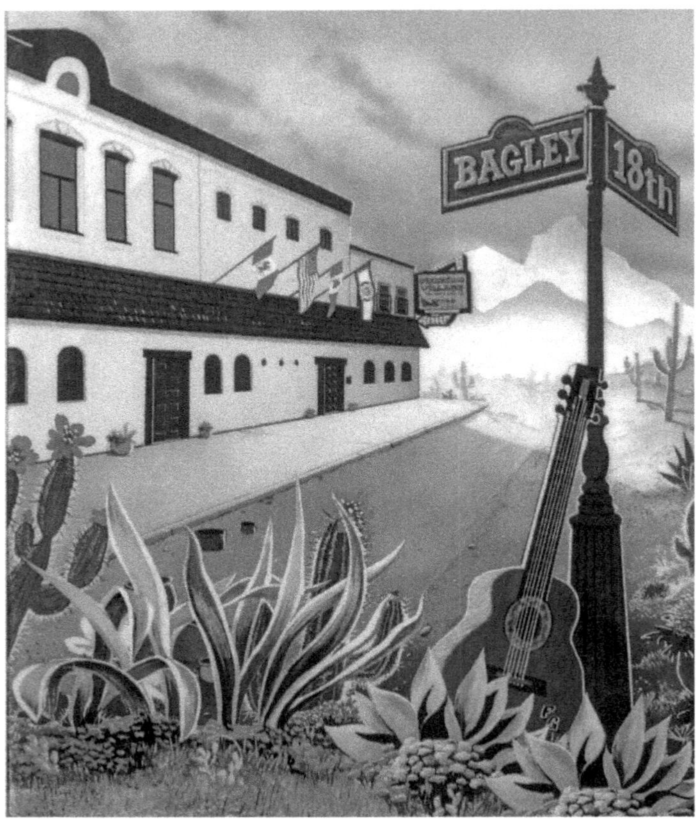

The cover of Mexican Village's menu depicts the building in very different surroundings. *Courtesy of the author, with thanks to Connie Bacigalupo.*

Like many neighborhoods in Detroit, Mexicantown was affected by unwelcome changes following the 1967 insurrection, but unlike other areas, it managed to maintain a strong resiliency. Today, the strip of Bagley Avenue from Eighteenth to Twenty-Fourth Street remains the heart of Detroit's Latino community, which includes restaurants serving Cuban and Guatemalan cuisine.

Mexican Village continues to attract a diverse crowd of patrons from all around metro Detroit and represents a true community fixture. Many employees are the second or even third generation of their families to work at the restaurant, a testimony to the family atmosphere Connie strives to maintain. In explaining her philosophy, she simply says, "When you have a family business, you put your heart into it."

15

Polynesian

Mauna Loa

There are basically two types of ethnic restaurants. The first kind are reflected in an image of a Chinese immigrant starting a Chinese restaurant or of a new arrival from Germany opening a neighborhood rathskeller. The second variety are places begun by investors who research upcoming trends, spot a style of cuisine that promises to be the new rage and take a chance on the idea. The people behind the latter are usually not of the given ethnic group themselves.

Most ethnic restaurants in Detroit hew pretty closely to the first model. One exception, however, was Mauna Loa, an ambitious undertaking on West Grand Boulevard near Woodward Avenue.

In the late 1960s, the Polynesian culture suddenly became quite popular. A group of local figures (mostly sports figures and attorneys) pooled their resources and constructed the freestanding restaurant, named after an active volcano on the island of Hawaii. The entrepreneurs spared no expense, spending $1.6 million on the project—an unheard-of amount at the time. The building was intentionally windowless, part of an effort to transport the patron to a magical South Seas paradise. The *New Center News* ran an article shortly after the opening that vividly described the interior:

> *Nearly every detail of its island décor was imported from Hawaii, even the rocks and carved wooden posts. Five main dining areas have walls and ceilings covered with basket woven straw, and floors covered with floral carpeting. The visitor has*

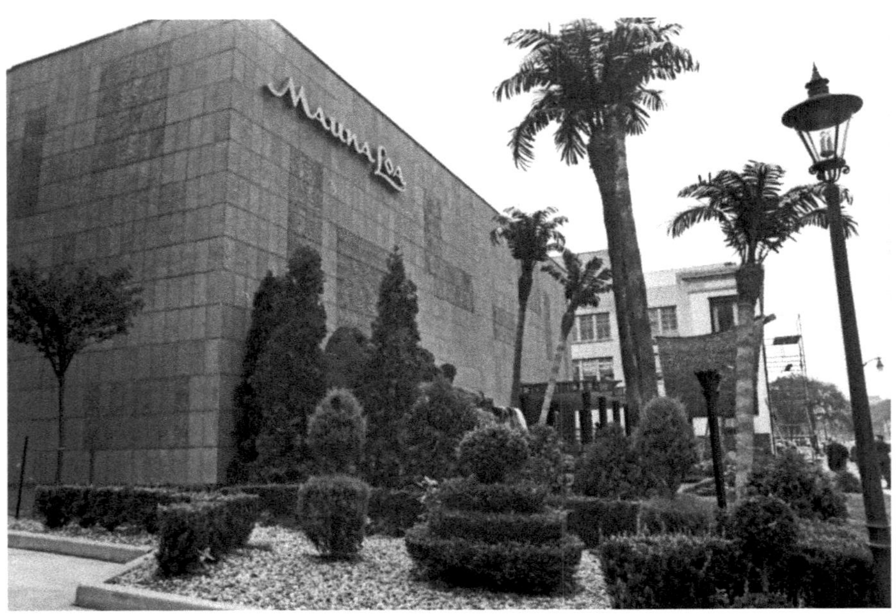

One of Detroit's contributions to the Polynesian trend of the late 1960s was Mauna Loa, a culinary and visual treat both inside and out. *Courtesy of the Walter Reuther Library.*

> *the impression that he actually is in a large thatched hut. The entrance is designed like an old ship, to convey the idea that the patron is going on an "island cruise." To walk from one room to another, it is necessary to cross a small bridge over a stream, for there are seven waterfalls in the Mauna Loa. There is also a deep pool where a Polynesian girl dives for pearls as patrons watched.*

Despite the clearly defined cultural milieu, the offerings at the Mauna Loa were fairly eclectic. Expected entrées, such as lau (steamed boneless pork, chicken or beef salted and wrapped in taro or ti leaves) or huli huli chicken (grilled chicken halves flavored with soy sauce, pineapple juice, brown sugar, ginger, garlic and wine), shared menu space with more customary American and European favorites. Mixed drinks were a strong part of the Mauna Loa experience, and the lead bartender was proficient in mixing a wide variety of rum-based cocktails.

But despite the elaborate presentation, the Mauna Loa's popularity proved to be fleeting. Closed after a run of just two years, the building later became the new home of The Clam Shop before succumbing to a fire, resulting in its demolition. Today, the site is occupied by an expansion of the nearby St. Regis Hotel.

Trader Vic's

By the late 1960s, tiki-themed bars and restaurants had become the rage around the nation. But Victor "Trader" Bergeron, who ran a sandwich shop in Oakland, California, saw the trend coming years earlier and seized it with gusto. In 1934, Bergeron traveled down the coast to Los Angeles, where he met a fellow who called himself Don the Beachcomber. Don ran a restaurant near the beach that offered seafood and libations with a Polynesian twist. Victor (who was given the nickname "Trader" due to his business acumen) had always wanted to run a higher-end establishment. He studied Don's place and decided that he could "build a better mousetrap."

Upon returning to Oakland, Victor did an extensive renovation of his place (with the quirky name "Hinky Dinks") and reopened under the name "Trader Vic's." His new concept was a hit, and soon he expanded the concept nationwide. Detroit's edition opened in 1969 in what had been the Café Rouge in the Detroit Statler-Hilton hotel (previously the Hotel Statler) on Washington Boulevard.

By the late 1960s, the old hotel had surely seen better days, and it was little secret that the national chain was brought in to help shore up its fortunes. But the underlying reason notwithstanding, Trader Vic's offered something

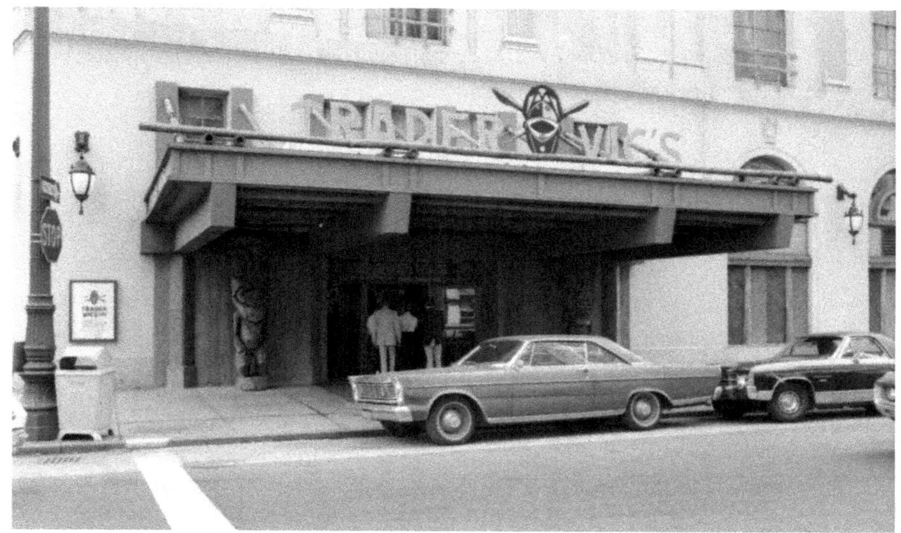

Trader Vic's was Detroit's edition of a popular national chain of Polynesian restaurants. Opened in the early 1960s in the Statler Hotel, the eatery was unable to reverse the hotel's fortunes. *Courtesy of the Walter Reuther Library.*

fairly unique to the midwestern diner. Dishes with exotic-sounding names from seaside locations of South Pacific and the Caribbean like abalone Kowloon, sweet and pungent fish and Ginko chicken tempted customers. Any good restaurateur knew that the old American standbys were necessary to placate the less adventurous diner. Victor was sure to include them, but with a South Seas packaging. A section of the menu headed "Meats from My Chinese Oven" included Indonesian lamb roast and barbecued suckling pig.

"You feed your belly at home, we give you a place where you can feed your belly and dine," Victor was fond of saying.

But elaborate beverages were also an important part of the Trader Vic's brand. Drinks invented by company bartenders sported exotic names like the Barbados Cocktail, Missionary's Revenge or the Trader Vic's Rum Cup and were dispensed from the extravagantly decorated bar. In fact, Trader Vic's claimed to have invented the famous Mai Tai.

Trader Vic's did good business for several years in the Hilton, but if the aim was to restore the hotel to prosperity, the effort fell short. While the restaurant did reasonably well, the hotel's financial health nosedived. By 1975, the hotel occupancy rate had plummeted to an average of just 20 percent, destroying any hope of profitability. In October of that year, the utilities were cut off, forcing it—and Trader Vic's—to close.

Although the popularity of the Polynesian theme of dining has waxed and waned over the years, Trader Vic's has managed to maintain its footing. Today, Victor Bergeron's descendants run the company and have found new markets in Africa and the Middle East.

TOP OF THE FLAME

Newspaper reviews covering the opening of the Top of the Flame from April 1963 reveal some telling facts—not just about the new restaurant but about the city as well.

Surprising at it may seem, until that time, Detroit lacked a dining spot located on the top of a high-rise building. But when the sleek new headquarters of Michigan Consolidated Gas Company opened a year earlier, the event represented a watershed moment for Detroit. The new modern tower, designed in the International Style by celebrated architect Minoru Yamasaki, represented a new postwar prosperity, prompting the building's owners to take a cue from other major cities. The building was

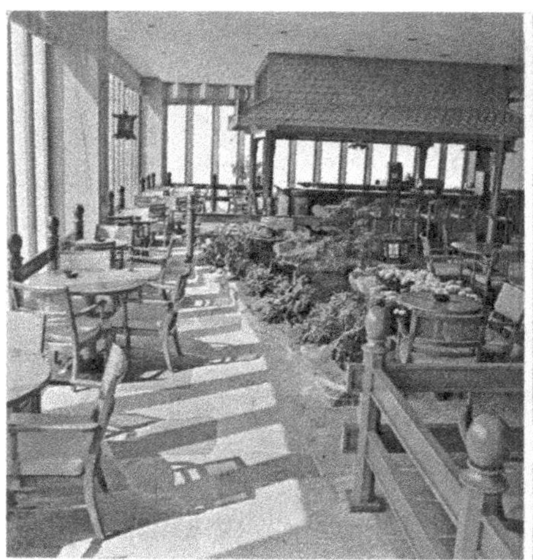

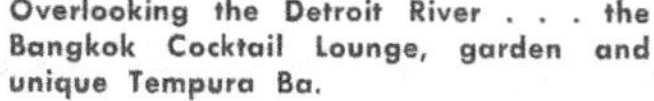

Overlooking the Detroit River . . . the Bangkok Cocktail Lounge, garden and unique Tempura Ba.

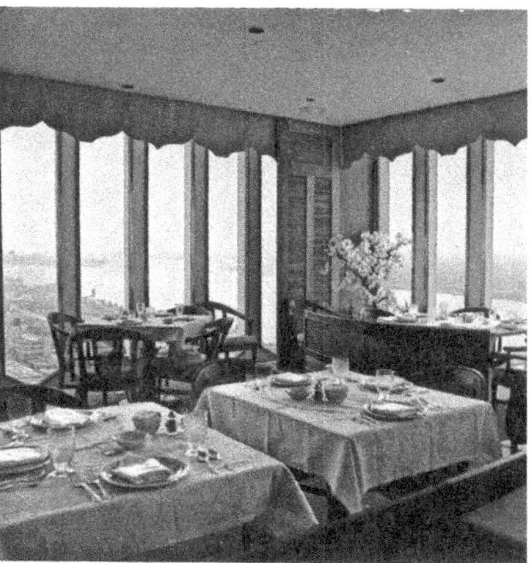

One of many beautiful views from the "Top" . . . Belle Isle and east toward the St. Clair River.

The dining room at the Top of the Flame, Detroit's first restaurant sporting a panoramic view. *Courtesy of the Walter Reuther Library.*

filled with allusions to its purpose as home of a natural gas company. The outdoor reflecting pools were punctuated with small gas jets displaying blue flames, and the light fixtures on the thirty-foot lobby ceiling each had a small blue bulb in the center.

The Stouffer Company, already well represented in Detroit, was hired to design and manage the venue. Stouffer's had developed an affection for running restaurants atop high-rise buildings, incorporating that fact into their names, such as the Top of the Marine in Milwaukee and the Top of the Mart in Atlanta.

For its Detroit venture, an Asian motif was selected, with the extensive décor including Thai, Korean and Japanese themes. The stunning architecture of the building combined with the engaging interior charmed the public, as a review in the *Detroit Free Press* revealed:

> *You walk across a lustrous white marble floor to the elevator, and it whisks you to the 26th floor in seconds. When the doors open, you step into another world—actually a copy of a classic residence in Bangkok, embellished by the ancient arts of Thailand. Teakwood walls, vermilion carpet and five-foot crystal chandelier like a shower of raindrops give you an immediate welcome in the entrance lounge*

> *Here a carved wooden Tepanom (angel figure) greets you with the Thai gesture of clapped hands.*

A review in the *Detroit News* praised the previously unavailable view: "The view is sheer soul medicine; at night the river forms a silvery ribbon between Detroit and Windsor with city lights twinkling into suburbia. It's as spectacular as Paris seen from night skies." Capitalizing on the daytime view, Stouffer's printed napkins featuring a map of downtown Detroit, with key landmarks labeled for customers to identify.

Surprisingly, however, the menu was predominately American. Steaks, chops and a few fish choices composed the bulk of the menu, punctuated by only a few Chinese and Thai favorites.

Part III

Let's Do Lunch: Casual Spots Around the City

"Hey, let's grab some lunch" is a suggestion often heard between Detroiters of all stripes: co-workers, business associates, neighbors and friends. Today, sadly, the venue for the noontime meal is often a chain fast-food outlet. Historically, of course, this is a recent development. In the not too distant past, lunch was enjoyed in variety of places—fine restaurants, diners and cafeterias, just to name a few.

During World War II, many Americans' lives were radically altered, creating unpredictable work schedules and a greater demand for restaurant meals, especially at lunchtime. In 1943, the federal government gave citizens an incentive to eat out when it declared that meals taken in restaurants would be exempt from personal wartime rationing. The downside was that special rules applied to the restaurateurs regarding the foods they could purchase. Meats and fish were often absent from the menu—resulting in choices heavy with pastas and salads.

Historic photos of downtown streetscapes from the 1930s and 1940s often feature signs emblazoned with just the word "LUNCH" above the entrance of an otherwise anonymous eatery. But despite this apparent uniformity, each maintained its distinct personality. In an era before cookie-cutter chain outlets, it was easier to feel what architects like to call "a sense of place"—a feeling of personal security that comes with being anchored in clearly identifiable surroundings. In the downtown Detroit of the 1940s and 1950s, many of the ubiquitous lunch spots offered this.

Today, some of these casual restaurants survive but hide unexpected secrets. In Hamtramck, the current site of the Polonia restaurant was a Depression-era eatery known as the Workingmen's Co-op restaurant. According to the online newspaper *Model D*, it was "a Depression era luncheonette favored by members of the Hamtramck Communist Party, which ran a full slate of candidates in the 1936 city elections."

Back then, in an era prior to drive-thru windows and supersize fries, enjoying lunch in unique surroundings made it less of a routine experience and more of a punctuation mark dividing the day in two. No doubt the respite made both halves more tolerable.

And since everyone has to eat lunch, why not do it in a place more memorable?

16

American Coney Island

The longer a restaurant is around, the greater the number of folk tales and urban legends it inspires. American Coney Island, an anchor to the downtown business district, is a textbook case in point. The owner, the exuberant Grace Keros, loves to set the record straight. "My grandfather Gus Keros emigrated from Greece in 1917 and landed at Ellis Island. His destination was Detroit, where he hoped to find work. But when he arrived, he wasn't able get [a job], so he decided to become self-reliant."

Gus began with a simple pushcart, which he operated from the corner of where the restaurant now sits. He sold popcorn and hot dogs, as well as shined shoes and cleaned hats. Soon the adjacent storefront became available, and Gus rented the space to start a small lunch spot. When deciding what to serve, Gus recalled that while in New York, he had briefly visited the famous Coney Island amusement park and enjoyed its hot dogs. Soon he came up with the idea of serving chili, onions and mustard over a hot dog, adopting elements from Greek culinary traditions. The New York connection prompted him to name his new creation a "Coney Island." The concept was a hit with Detroit diners, and Gus expanded the menu to include the now familiar loose hamburgers, Greek salads and gyros sandwiches. In 1924, Gus brought his brother Bill over from Greece, who emulated his brother's success by opening his restaurant, Lafayette Coney Island, next door.

For decades, a number of urban legends have circulated regarding the "Coney Wars"—or American versus Lafayette. One suggests that the two brothers opened one restaurant together, had a knockdown, drag-out

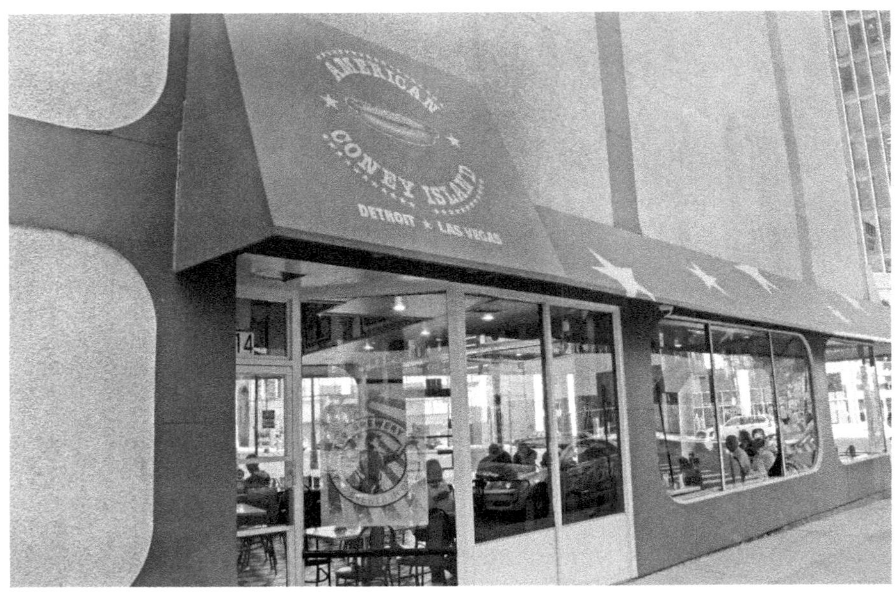

One of Detroit's claims to culinary fame, the American Coney Island. Note the names of both Detroit and Las Vegas on the awning. *Courtesy of the author, with thanks to Grace Keros.*

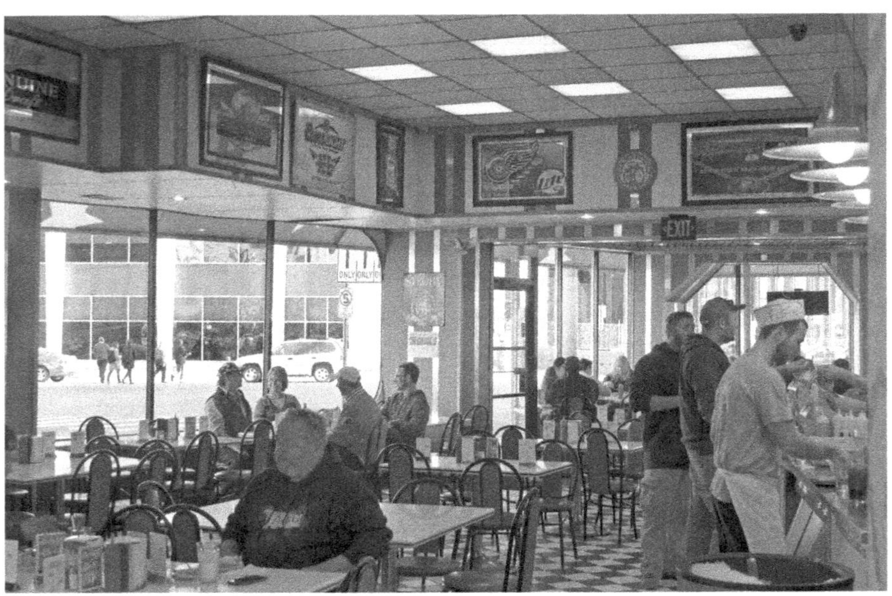

Open twenty-four hours a day, American offers a continuous window on urban life from its location at the confluence of Michigan Avenue, Griswold Street and Lafayette Boulevard. *Courtesy of the author, with thanks to Grace Keros.*

argument and sliced the establishment in two, each for one person to run. Although there has been a long-standing rivalry between the two, Grace explains that the story is nothing more than chopped hamburger.

What is painfully evident, however, is the intense conflict of loyalties between customers of the two establishments. In Detroit, American versus Lafayette arouses passions similar to rivalries like East Side versus West Side, Michigan versus Michigan State or the state's Lower Peninsula versus its Upper Peninsula.

The classic diner-style interior— "tastefully tacky," as Grace affectionately puts it, is clearly visible through the large windows on the unusually shaped building, which resembles a piece of pie pointing toward the three-way intersection of Michigan Avenue, Griswold Street and Lafayette Boulevard in the heart of downtown. The atypical location makes the restaurant an engaging window on urban life, where diners can visit at any time, as the restaurant is open twenty-four hours a day, 365 days a year. Over the years, Hollywood has taken note of the American. To date, scenes from fourteen major motion pictures and two scenes from the TV cop drama *Detroit 187* have been filmed there.

Decades of notoriety have paid off for Grace and her family. Loyal fans who have moved to distant parts of the country (and world) can order American Coney dog "kits" by phone or online and have them shipped from the restaurant's warehouse in suburban Detroit. Sporting the snappy title "Send a Taste of Detroit," the kit contains all the essential ingredients, which come packed in dry ice and require minimal preparation. Grace also offers the kits at a discounted rate to nonprofits as a fundraising tool.

The still thriving restaurant continues to operate today under the same family's ownership, with Grace representing its third generation. The chili used is homemade from a secret recipe developed by Gus Keros almost a century ago. "American"—as intimates refer to it—is a major gathering spot for professional athletes, journalists and celebrities, both local and national.

But perhaps American Coney Island's biggest claim to fame is its location at the D Hotel in Las Vegas. The Detroit-themed hotel, opened in 2012 was the first American location (and one of the few Coney Islands of any brand) outside Michigan to offer the same mouthwatering food as the original. Even the décor is the same.

One of the few changes at the Detroit location was to the awning over the entrance. It reads, "American Coney Island—Detroit–Las Vegas."

17

Buddy's Pizza

The storied restaurant's website sets the scene perfectly: "Six Mile Road and Conant Avenue was like any street corner in Detroit, Philadelphia or New York…people walking to the market, children playing stickball in the street, neighbors helping neighbors, and friends meeting at the local gathering spot now known as Buddy's." That was in 1936, when Buddy's opened as a clandestine bar in a heavily Italian east side neighborhood. Prohibition had recently ended, but "blind pigs"—drinking establishments that skirted laws regarding alcohol consumption—were still commonplace. About a decade later, August "Gus" Guerra, Buddy's proprietor, converted the place to a legitimate bar and restaurant. At the same time, his cook, Connie Piccinato, added a unique version of Sicilian square deep-dish pizza to the menu that became an instant hit. Knowing the idea was a winner, two friends from the neighborhood, Jimmy Bonacorse and Jimmy Valenti, bought Buddy's and its phenomenal pizza recipe in 1953.

The new creation attracted quite a crowd, making Buddy's a neighborhood gathering spot. Groups of regulars came to drink, eat and play Italian card games brought over from the old country. Arguments between old Italian men would often result, creating a cacophony of insults—usually screamed in their native tongue. Concerned about the sensibilities of the other customers, the owners eventually expanded the building to include a separate card room for the older crowd.

Buddy's Italian character extended outside the building as well. For decades, the restaurant has hosted bocce ball tournaments on Saturdays

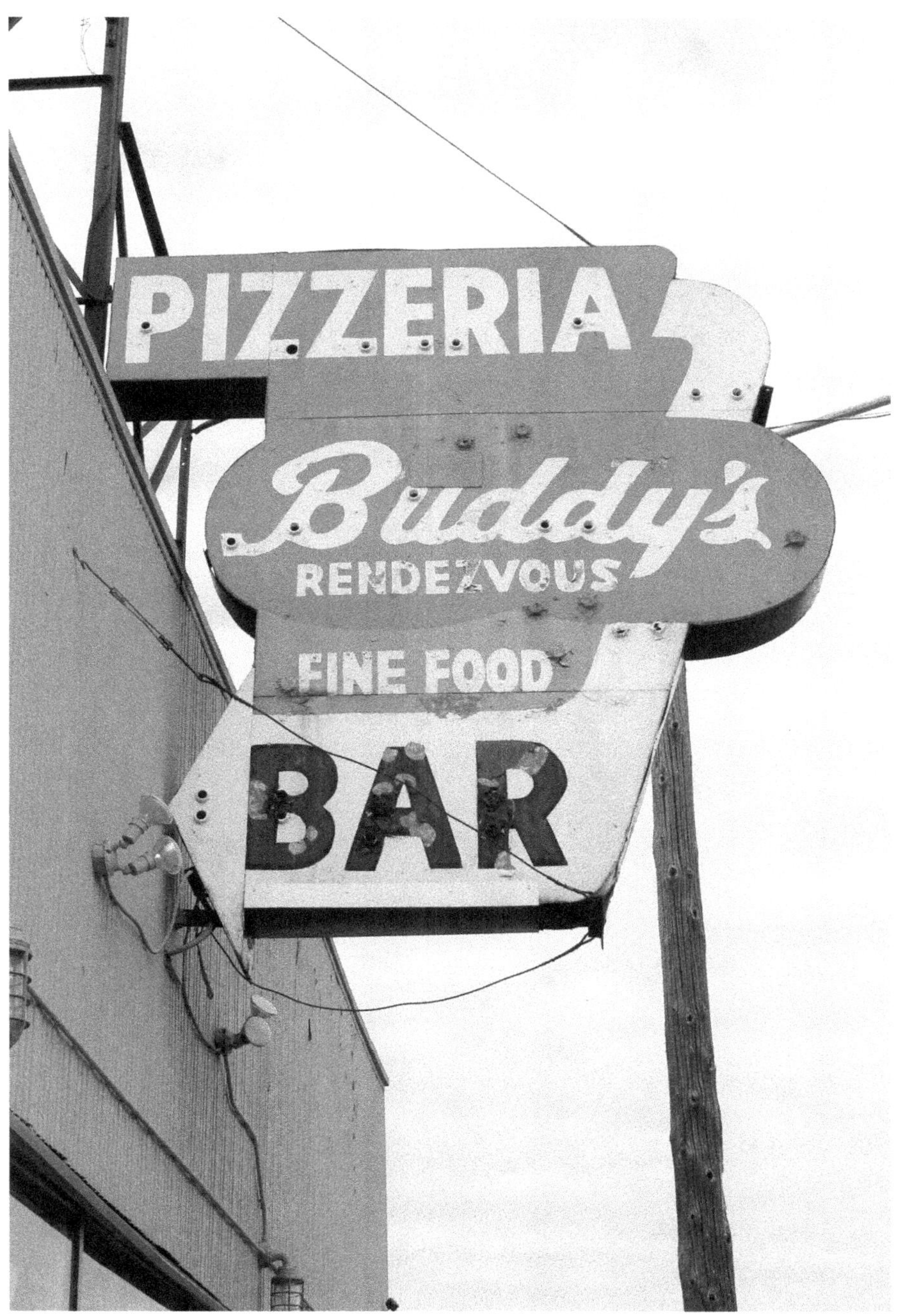

A 2016 view of the circa 1955 sign at the original Buddy's at Conant Street and Six Mile Road. *Courtesy of the author, with thanks to Buddy's Pizza.*

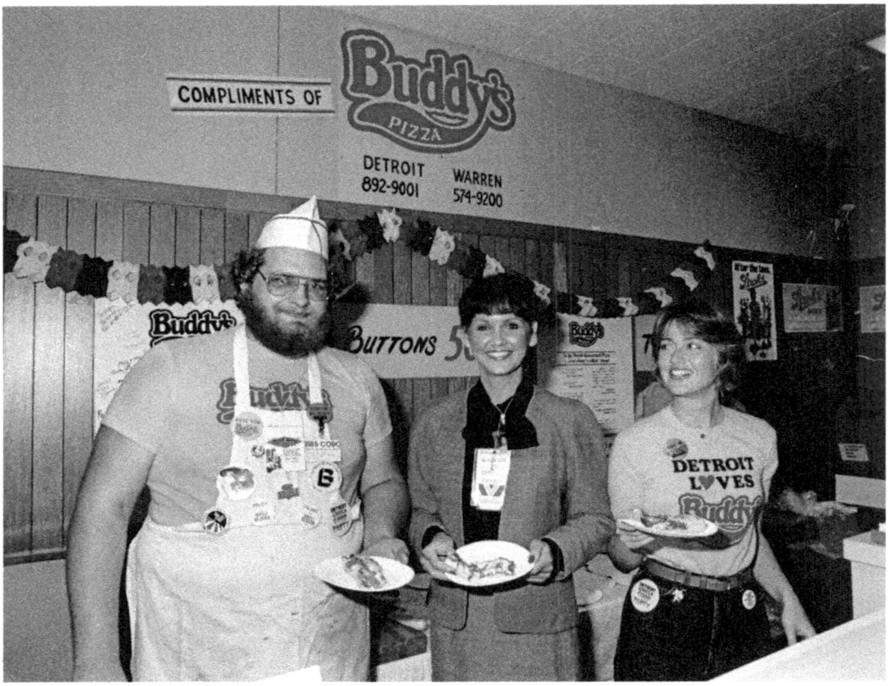

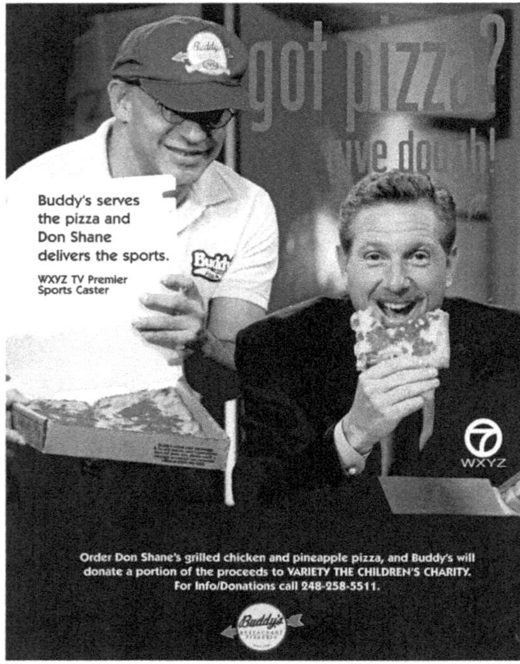

Above: Buddy's Pizza, another Detroit original, consistently attracts a wide and diverse clientele, including businesspeople and convention-goers from out of town. *Courtesy of Buddy's Pizza.*

Left: Always a supporter of local charities, Buddy's has long enlisted local celebrities to help out, including WXYZ sportscaster Don Shane. *Courtesy of Buddy's Pizza.*

during the warm-weather months. A game imported from Italy, bocce ball can best be described as a cross between bowling and shuffleboard. Players take turns bowling a bocce ball the length of a court with the object of having it stop as close as possible to a spot predetermined by the initial throw of a smaller ball, the jack, known as the *boccino* or *pallino* in Italian.

A 1977 article in the *Detroit Free Press* pointed out some of the characteristics that set the game apart:

> *The Courts at Buddy's are about 30 yards long, though the game can be played at a minimum of 26 yards. Most courts are 8 to 13 feet wide.*
>
> *Though the basic rules are quite simple, the game is more challenging than its counterparts like horseshoes or shuffleboard. In bocce, there are more variables because of the dirt playing surface and a target that is not stationary. The boccino can get knocked around in an area about 10 yards long, and often is for reasons of strategy.*
>
> *One thing that makes it popular for the older players is that youth has little or no advantage. "It's one game where age doesn't really affect the player," said Charley Rivetto. At some sessions at Buddy's 80 and 85-year-old players take part.*

Within every popular restaurant category, there is almost always intense disagreement over which source of a given item ranks supreme. Pizza in Detroit stands out as a towering exception to this rule. On this score, Buddy's has occupied the number-one spot for decades and still enjoys this distinction today. In 2009, *GQ* magazine included Buddy's pizzas on its list of the nation's top twenty-five pizzas. In 2015, when Paul McCartney played the Fox Theatre, Buddy's sent over a slew of vegetarian pies. Buddy's pizza is consistently chosen by agents representing visiting celebrities to feed hungry stage crews.

Buddy's adheres to the familiar notion of quality over quantity. In a city rife with hundreds of places offering cheap, mass-produced "pies," as they're known in the industry, none can quite match the delicious Buddy's formula: a blend of bread, cheese and sauce baked to achieve just the right consistency and deliver the unmistakable Buddy's flavor. Bob Talbert, a longtime columnist for the *Detroit Free Press*, once wrote, "Is Buddy's the best pizza? It sure is, because it is the one that all the others are compared to."

Today, Buddy's operates out of eleven Detroit-area locations, including the original at Six Mile and Conant Streets. In addition to the pizza (which is offered in several variations, including gluten free), you'll find burgers, an array of sandwich choices and one of the best minestrone soups anywhere.

In 1970, Buddy's was sold to William and Shirlee Jacobs, who soon began opening suburban locations. And although these satellites sport funky interiors and the same delicious creations at the Detroit mothership, there's nothing like a visit to the original.

18

The Clam Shop

Sadly, 2675 East Grand Boulevard is now just a vacant lot. But from the mid-1950s until 1975, the site was the location of a much-beloved seafood restaurant, The Clam Shop. Recognized as a more moderately priced alternative to Joe Muer's, The Clam Shop drew much of its clientele from the surrounding industrial environs. Originally called the Milwaukee Junction, the area was the home of some of the very earliest automotive factories, including the Ford Piquette Plant and the first home of Oakland Motors (later-day Pontiac). By midcentury, the neighborhood was a plethora of machine, tool and die shops supplying the nearby assembly plants.

The Clam Shop served white and blue collar alike, with hearty portions of broiled red snapper, fried frog legs and soft shell crabs. And for the non-fish lover, there was sirloin steak—as a full dinner or à la carte.

The management of The Clam Shop was especially dedicated to customer satisfaction. A note on a vintage menu tells the customer: "Any complaint in food or personnel should be reported to the management. We would appreciate it." Immediately below appears a welcome compliment— "The correct wine is the wine of your choice."

The Clam Shop had a successful run until 1975. That year, an industrialist from the area bought the restaurant and moved it down the street to the site of the Mauna Loa, which had closed some years earlier. The old location was thought to be too small, and the new owner believed that larger quarters would allow the restaurant to host larger crowds.

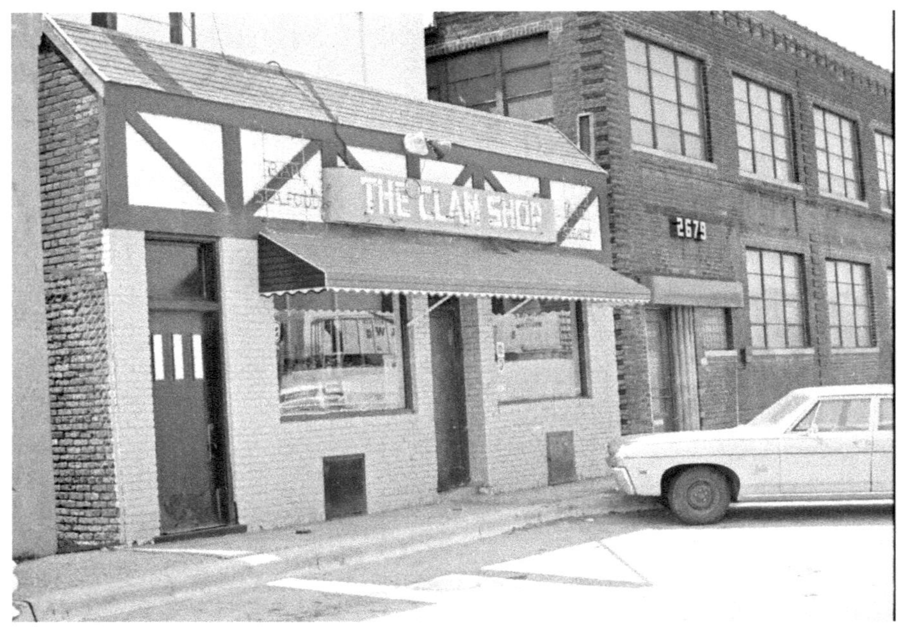

A 1960s view of The Clam Shop at 2675 East Grand Boulevard. *Courtesy of the Walter Reuther Library.*

But when the old Mauna Loa closed up, much of the Polynesian décor was left behind. A review in the *Detroit Free Press* shortly after the move pointed out the strange juxtaposition: "By what has to be something of a minor miracle, much of the original décor survived the long dormancy of the place. With the exception of the handsome tables, and such not particularly missed touches as blowfish lamps, little seems to have been altered. Detroit has a Polynesian seafood house…Aloha, Clam Shop."

Unfortunately, the move did not foster success. Only a year later, the new owner fell behind on his loan payments, and the bank threatened foreclosure. Less than a week before the restaurant was slated to be padlocked, a mysterious fire broke out that was later determined to be an act of arson. The owner implicated a group of younger patrons who, after an altercation with management, allegedly threated to burn the establishment down, but a reasonable person might tend to arrive at an alternate theory. The investigation proved inconclusive, however, and no one was ever charged.

19

Darby's

The postwar years brought mobility to Detroit and the nation. Areas previously thought to be "in the sticks"—even if they lay technically with in the city limits—were being transformed into new neighborhoods built in the initial version of the suburban model. Little known today is that this phenomenon actually began on the outskirts of the city proper before crossing Eight Mile Road.

The Boesky family (known for their infamous namesake deli at Twelfth and Hazelwood Streets) took note of this trend when they opened Darby's at Seven Mile Road and Wyoming Avenue in 1955. Sam Boesky, who ran the bistro, explained to the *Detroit Times* in 1958 that the modern concept of a restaurant should have "something for everybody." He set up Darby's along a three-in-one model—"a small lunch counter for the quick coffee and sandwich, a coffee shop for those with a little more time, plus an elegant main room for sumptuous dining." Owing to the formality of the era, "sumptuous" meant just that. White tablecloths and stylish Midcentury Modern décor provided a comfortable setting for patrons. The menu was promoted as featuring "Jewish style cooking" with items that appealed to the largely Jewish clientele: white fish, chicken paprikash and gefilte fish. A number of standard American dishes rounded out the menu.

A centerpiece of the predominantly Jewish neighborhood, Darby's prided itself as a real community institution, sporting the slogan "the best of food with the best of people" in its advertising. Regular patrons could rest assured they'd run into a least one friend per visit.

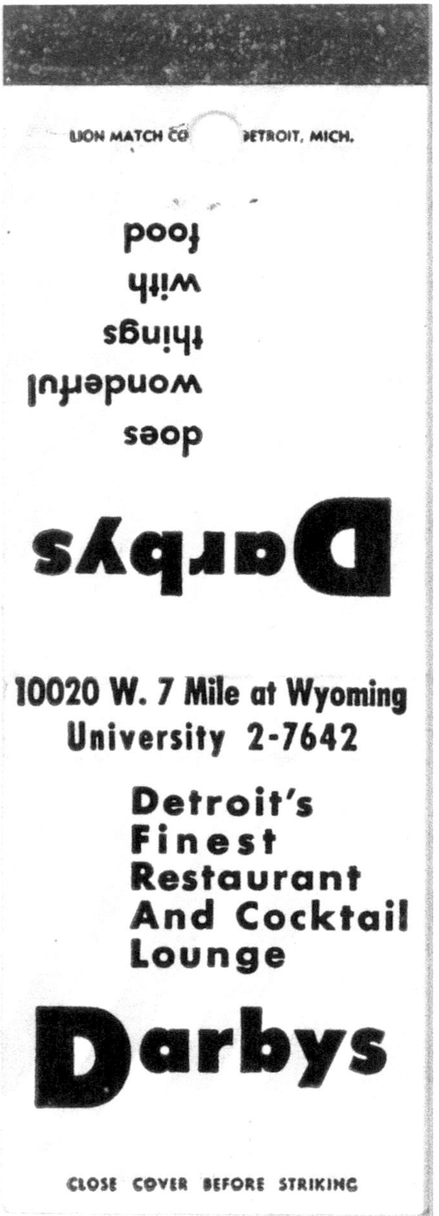

A vintage matchbook cover from Darby's a community fixture at the corner of Wyoming Avenue and Seven Mile Road. *Author's collection.*

The restaurant also did a strong catering business for all sorts of occasions and was known for the pastries produced by its in-house bakery. The restaurant was such a community institution that it even allowed regulars to dine on credit, with the staff mailing out monthly bills. Such trustworthiness is unthinkable today.

Darby's proudly served the northwest community for over a decade before it succumbed to an explosion and fire in July 1968. The fire was at first deemed suspicious, and police reported two cars speeding away along Wyoming Avenue immediately after the blaze began.

Not surprisingly, nearby residents viewed the fire as a great loss to the neighborhood and the end of an era, and time has proven them correct. The loss of Darby's represented a turning point in the neighborhood's downward spiral. Today, the intersection is home to a chain drugstore and a few gas stations. The area has lost much of its affluence and would no doubt be unable to support a restaurant of Darby's caliber if it were there today.

20

Greenfield's

Downtown types during the 1960s and 1970s—shoppers, office workers or people just kicking back for a day and looking for a good but not too expensive lunch—often headed to Greenfield's, a classic midcentury cafeteria. Greenfield's had two locations, one in the heart of downtown at Griswold and State Streets and another farther up Woodward Avenue at

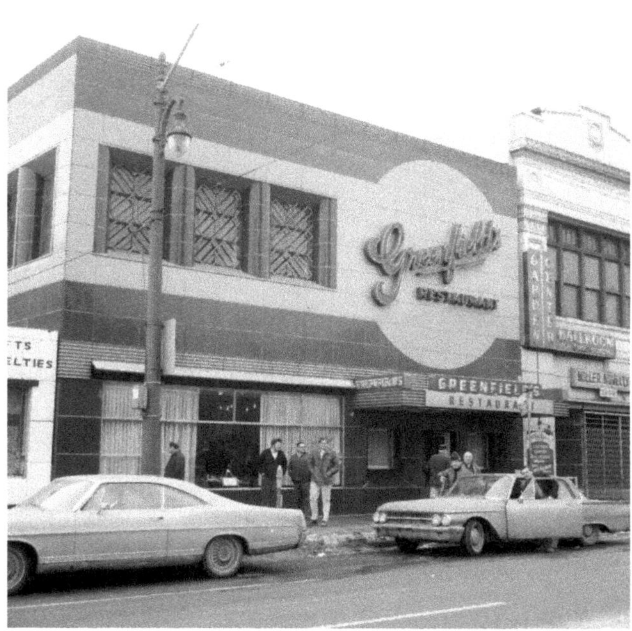

Greenfield's, a familiar downtown lunch spot, specialized in "comfort food" back in the early 1960s, before the term was coined. *Courtesy of the Walter Reuther Library.*

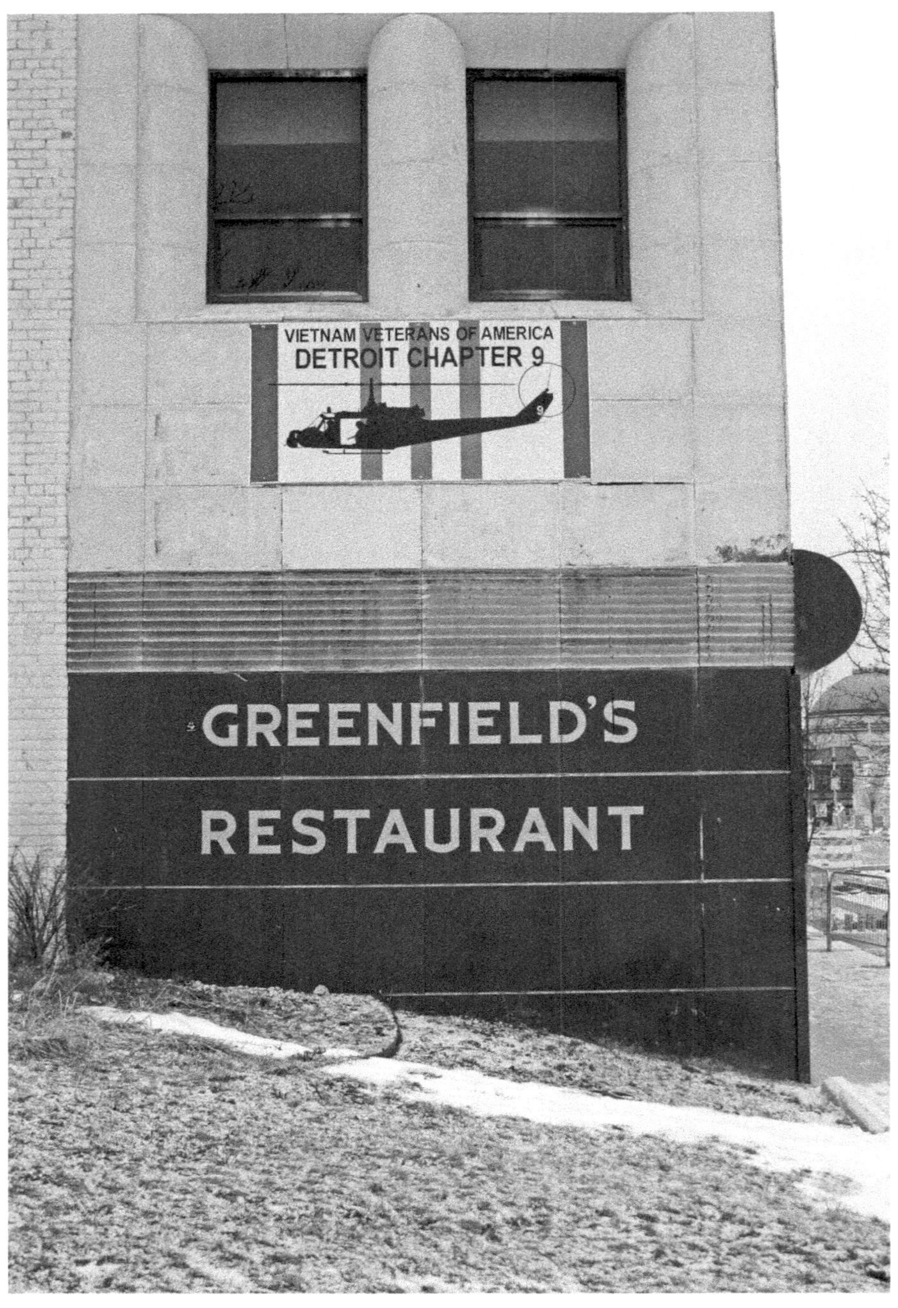

Greenfield's location at 2951 Woodward Avenue is now the home of the Detroit chapter of the Vietnam Veterans of America, but for some reason, the old sign remains. *Courtesy of the author.*

Temple Street. For a time, Greenfield's also operated the cafeteria in the basement of the City County Building.

Youngsters of the era fondly recall lunch at Greenfield's as part of a day spent downtown with a parent or grandparent that often included shopping and perhaps a movie at one of several palatial theaters.

One visitor to an online forum remarked, "My grandmother would often take me to the Greenfield's on Griswold after a morning of shopping at Hudson's and a 'ladies day' [Wednesday] matinee at one of the great old theaters. I loved the chopped steak and rice pudding!"

Greenfield's gradually became a fixture in different corners of metro Detroit. Suburban locations opened in Oak Park just across from Northland, along with a slightly more upscale spot in Birmingham. During the 1970s and 1980s, however, the cafeteria model fell out of fashion, resulting in Greenfield's ultimate demise. But one noteworthy reminder remains. Today, the building housing the one-time location at Woodward and Temple still sports the Greenfield's sign, one of many "ghost signs" (outdoor advertisements promoting long-extinct businesses) scattered around the city.

21

Hudson's Restaurants

Reflecting on the J.L. Hudson store—that mammoth, two-million-square-foot jewel from downtown's past—will bring a torrent of emotions to any Detroiter aged fifty-five and over. The second-largest department store in the nation, Hudson's was known for being more than just a store. Besides offering everything from clothing to appliances and garden supplies, it was a place for women to get their hair done, for men to get their hats cleaned and for anyone to enjoy looking at stunning works of art in the gallery or a meal at any of several in-store dining options. On the thirteenth floor were three luxurious dining rooms: the Pine Room, the Georgian Room and the Early American Room, which, after renovation in the early 1960s, became known as the Riverview Room.

Scattered elsewhere throughout the building were a snack bar and juice bar, and in the basement was a cafeteria where a student at Cass Technical High School named Diana Ross took a job as a busgirl in the early 1960s.

The tradition of in-store dining developed early in the company's history and followed Hudson's as it expanded into the suburbs beginning in the 1950s. Fortunately, it remains strong today despite several corporate mergers and the disappearance of the Hudson name. Today, almost all suburban Detroit locations of Macy's (Hudson's successor company) are home to a sit-down restaurant, branded today as The Lakeshore Grill.

The menu offered at Hudson's was classic American and included mouthwatering delicacies like Canadian cheese soup, Greek feta salad, hearty hot roast beef sandwiches and sour cream sugar cookies. In addition,

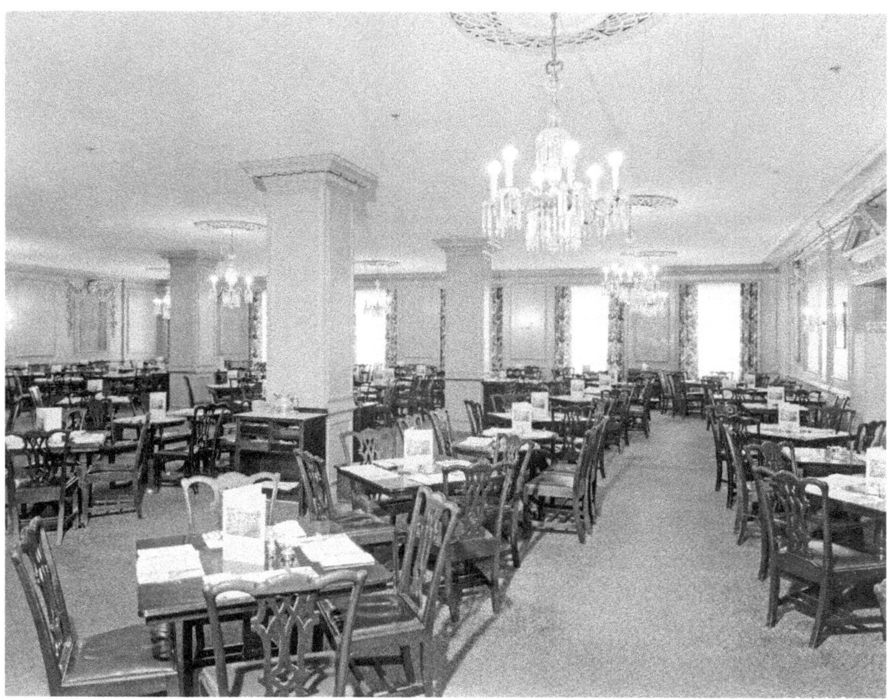

Above: Dining at downtown Hudson's, for lunch of dinner was a very special experience. This image is a view of the Colonial Dining Room on the thirteenth floor of the venerable department store. *Courtesy of the Davis Hillmer Collection/Detroit Historical Society (DHS).*

Right: A Hudson's menu dated October 27, 1949. *Courtesy of the Davis Hillmer Collection*/DHS.

Soups and Appetizers

Shrimp Cocktail	.45	Jellied Consomme	.20
Fresh Fruit Cocktail	.25	Relish Tray	.35
Chicken Okra Soup	.20	Chilled Apple Juice	.15

Cream of Asparagus Soup .20

Molded Fresh Strawberry and Banana Salad .25

Please order by number

	A la Carte	Complete Luncheon
1. Pot Roast of Beef a la Mode with Oven Browned Potato and Corn on the Cob	1.10	1.45
2. Breast of Chicken Imperial with String Beans and French Fried Egg Plant	1.25	1.60
3. Ham and Cauliflower au Gratin	1.00	1.55
4. Fresh Vegetable Plate (String Beans, Oven Browned Potato, French Fried Egg Plant, Parsley Creamed Cabbage and Corn on the Cob)	.95	1.30
5. Chef's Salad Bowl with Sliced Tongue and Imported Swiss Cheese	1.10	1.45
6. Sunburst Fruit Wheel Salad	.90	1.25
7. Individual Chicken Pie with Fricassee Gravy	.90	1.25

Cherry Square, Poppy Seed, French OR Parker House Roll

Tea, Coffee or Milk

The above complete luncheons include soup or fruit cocktail, 20¢ dessert and beverage

***Shopper's Luncheon** $1.10*

Chicken Okra Soup OR Chilled Apple Juice

Veal Patty with Bacon and Parsley Creamed Cabbage
OR
Cantaloupe Ring Filled with Fruit Cottage Cheese Salad

Banana Cup Cake Topped with Crushed Raspberries OR
Lime Sherbet

Cherry Square, Poppy Seed, French OR
Parker House Roll

Tea, Coffee OR Milk

Detroit's Police Department asks everyone's help i

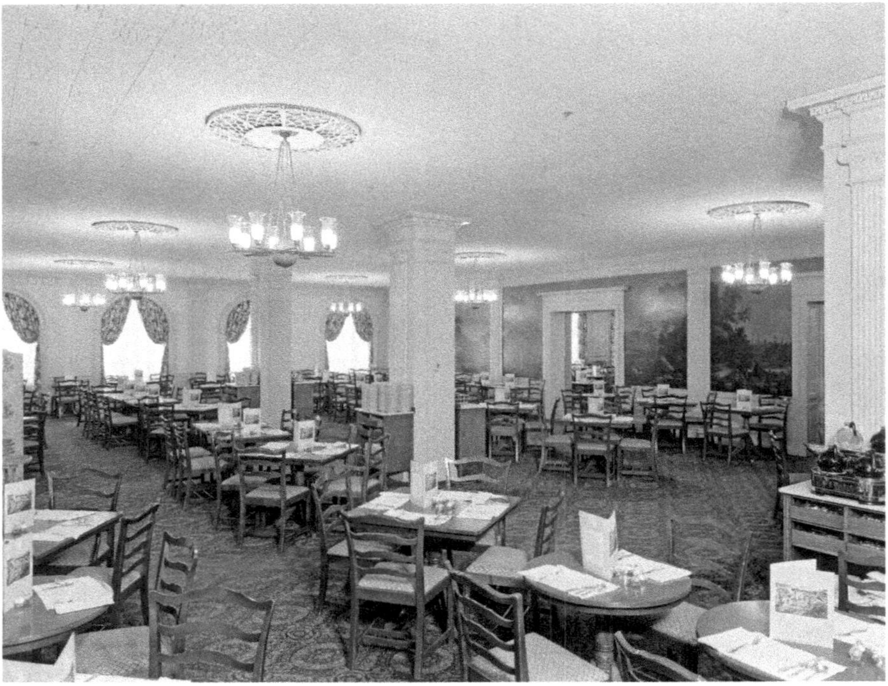

Above: Adjacent to the Colonial Room was the Early American Room. *Courtesy of the Davis Hillmer Collection/DHS.*

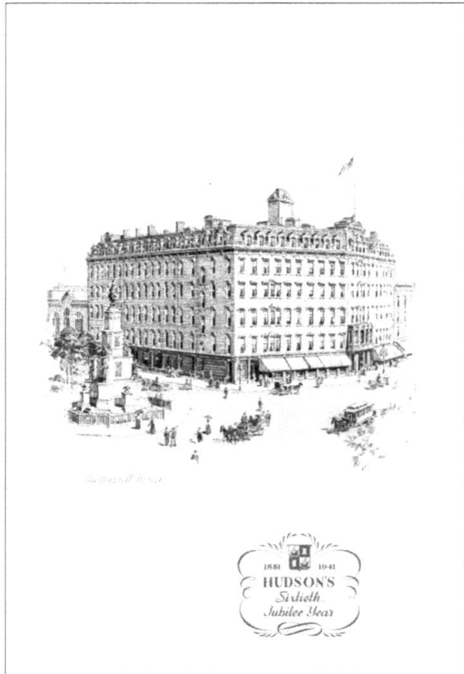

Left: An illustrated cover of a 1941 menu recognizing J.L. Hudson's sixtieth anniversary. The image is of the Russell House, an early Detroit hotel that stood near Campus Martius from 1836 until 1907. *Courtesy of the Davis Hillmer Collection/DHS.*

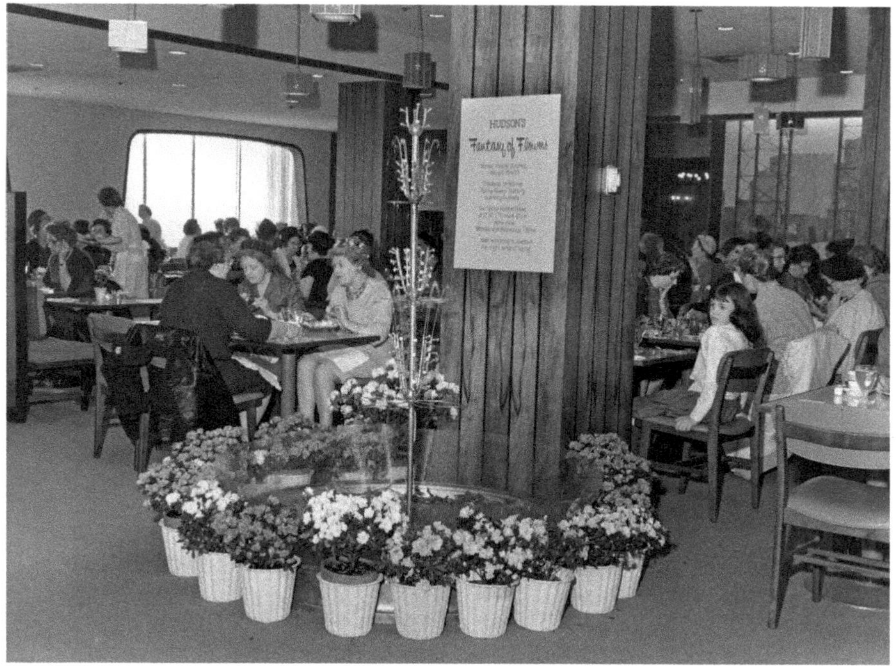

In 1959, the two rooms were combined, modernized and rebranded as the Riverview Room, featuring large windows to offer a view of the Detroit River. *Courtesy of the Davis Hillmer Collection/DHS.*

there were several items only available at Hudson's, such as the light bread popovers and the chicken pot pie. But the best known, of course, was the legendary Maurice Salad. For decades, the recipes for both the salad and the dressing were closely guarded company secrets.

But the glamour of dining at Hudson's was not always open to all, as the company harbored a none-too-subtle streak of racism. African American and Hispanic patrons often suffered slights like finding themselves in lines that never seemed to move. For years, blacks were not hired for sales or management positions. Backward attitudes persisted even outside the building, when black customers attempting to hail a cab on Woodward Avenue often experienced longer waits than did whites.

The mighty downtown store slowly contracted throughout the 1970s, as departments were closed and fake walls sectioned off unused floor space. The dining room, however, remained open until the store's very last day. Downtown Hudson's 1983 closing proved emotionally painful for many Detroiters, but the building's physical presence still provided some

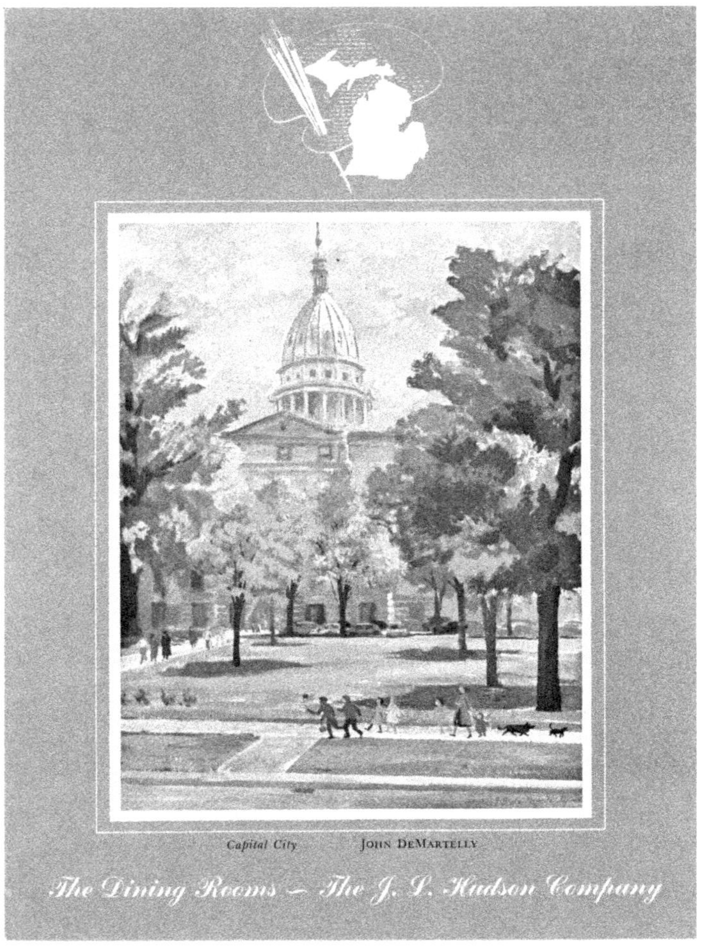

A Hudson's menu cover from the late 1940s showing a painting of the Michigan Capitol Building—part of Hudson's "Michigan on Canvas" series. *Courtesy of the Davis Hillmer Collection*/DHS.

solace. Its 1998 implosion caused utter heartbreak, an emotion that still tugs at Detroiters' heartstrings. Today, a stylish little bistro on Woodward just across from the Hudson's site is fittingly named the Hudson Café.

Today, new life appears to be coming to the old Hudson's site. At this writing, businessman Dan Gilbert, whose company recently acquired development rights to the site, announced plans for the construction of an impressive mixed-use high-rise that will offer additional apartments units to satisfy the high demand for downtown housing.

22

Lafayette Coney Island

Lafayette" as its loyalists simply refer to it, is the other side of Detroit's storied Coney Island rivalry. Opened by Bill Keros just a few years after his brother Gust started his restaurant, American Coney Island, Lafayette remains a downtown Detroit institution, just like its next-door counterpart. From the beginning, Bill decided to use a different recipe for the chili on his dogs, but the formula is otherwise the same: a natural casing hot dog served on a steamed bun with chili and often topped with mustard and chopped onions. Today, this original offering is complemented by chili by the bowl (with or without beans), loose hamburgers and chili cheese fries.

And also like its neighbor, Lafayette Coney Island has grown into a Detroit institution. Photos of Detroit and Michigan politicians adorn the walls, along with autographed portraits of local media personalities, images of noteworthy Detroit Tigers and Detroit Red Wings players and framed copies of newspapers announcing Stanley Cup and World Series victories. Following a victorious hockey season, even a replica Stanley Cup will be on display. Despite the exponential growth in the number of restaurants in the greater downtown area, Lafayette still enjoys the die-hard loyalty of its regulars. Walk in before any Tigers, Red Wings or Lions game, and you'll observe a sea of hometown jerseys.

Business is done at Lafayette just like it was fifty years ago. Walk in, sit down and choose from the *very* limited menu—Coney dogs, loose hamburgers, bean soup, chili with or without beans and chili cheese fries—then listen to the guy taking your order shout it unintelligibly to the people

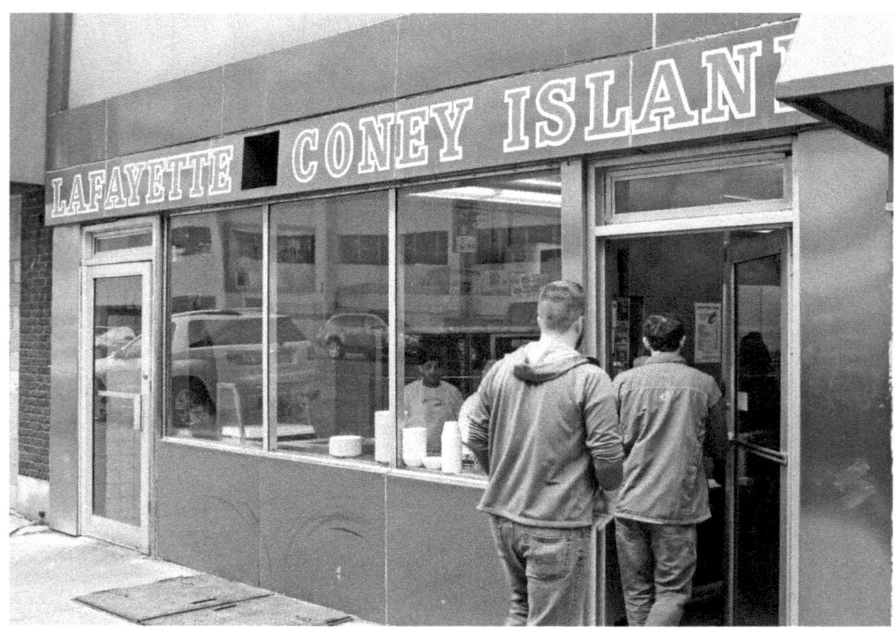

Rarely lacking for business, Lafayette Coney Island attracts patrons day and night. *Courtesy of the author.*

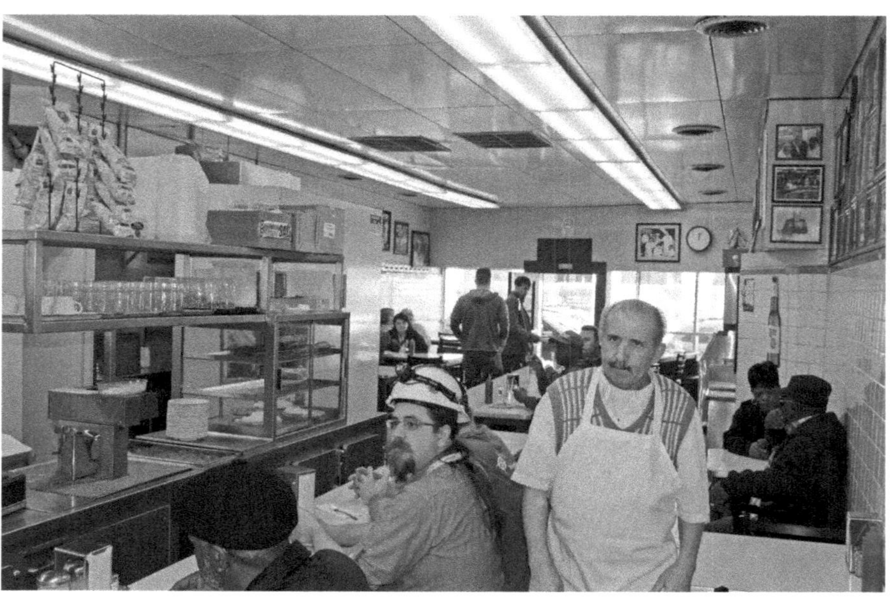

Aside from a few recent pictures on the walls, the interior of Lafayette looks frozen in the 1950s. *Courtesy of the author, with thanks to Lafayette Coney Island.*

in the exposed kitchen. About five minutes later, he drops it in front of you. When you're finished, he figures your bill in his head—nothing is ever written down. A well-weathered sign says, "Pay when served," but seasoned patrons know they don't need to—the policy changed years ago, but the staff never got around to taking it down. Seeing someone who does pay immediately is a sure way to spot a newbie.

In 1988, Bill Keros's descendants sold the business out of the family, but the transfer of ownership did nothing to erode its traditions. Today, Lafayette endures, strictly observing the formula set out by its founder.

23

The Money Tree

Picture a bustling sidewalk at midday in a busy downtown financial district. Well-dressed business people shuttled from point A to point B while traffic on the street is gridlocked. What do you need to complete the picture? A classy lunch spot where diners can view pedestrians and vice versa. For years, The Money Tree at the corner of Fort Street and Washington Boulevard served just that function.

Situated on the ground floor of a high-rise office tower, the modernly appointed restaurant attracted a daily draw of assorted white-collar types: stockbrokers, journalists from the two daily newspapers and attorneys—the latter often taking breaks from arguing cases at federal district court just across the street.

The clever name was a nod to the restaurant's Financial District location, an enclave of ornate, Neoclassical buildings clustered around Fort, Congress and Larned Streets that at one time was Detroit's answer to Wall Street. But the menu and ambiance reached back further—to eighteenth-century Detroit—and featured an array of French delicacies. The à la carte offerings included hors d'oeuvres, *salades* and entrées so authentic patrons would feel like they were magically transported to Paris. *Truite fumee* (smoked rainbow trout), *salade de la Maison* (Boston lettuce with pineapple, orange and almonds with celery seed dressing) and main courses like *tournedos de boeuf* (sautéed filet of beef tenderloin) and *carre d'agneau perillee* (lamb rack rolled in herbed bread crumbs) all competed for the diner's attention.

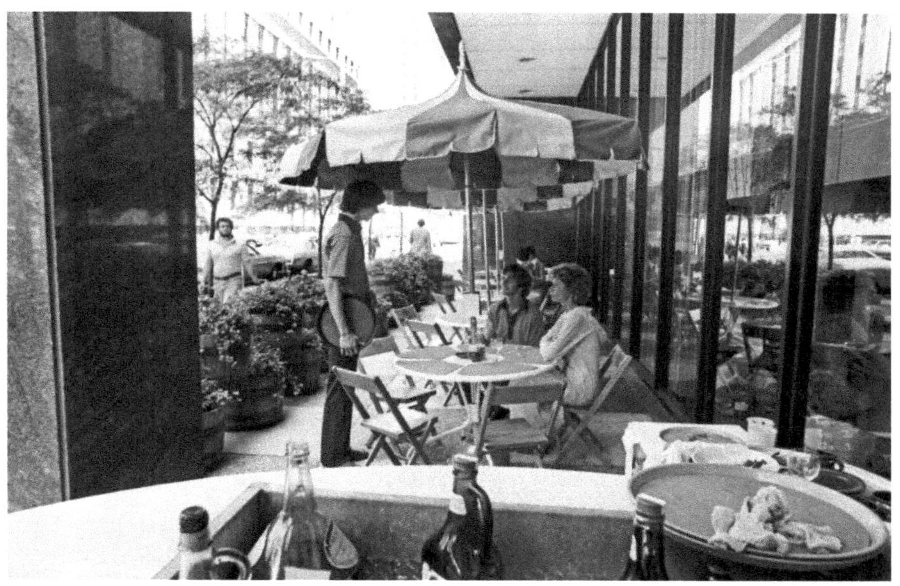

The Money Tree's sidewalk café, a summertime favorite, added a touch of class to downtown during the 1970s and 1980s. *Courtesy of the Walter Reuther Library.*

During its heyday in the 1980s, The Money Tree also offered upscale "power lunches" (the buzzword of the day)—Oriental London broil, duck pie and fancy chicken presentations. During the warm-weather months, the outdoor Café L'ete extended The Money Tree's elegance to the sidewalk along Fort Street. The delightful restaurant added a dash of style to the otherwise drab urban streetscape. Its closing in the late 1990s created a real void. Several new restaurants have opened in the core downtown of late, but none quite like The Money Tree.

24

Sanders

Chain establishments seldom achieve legendary status, but in Detroit, the name Sanders did, which placed it on equal footing with Coney dogs and Stroh's beer as regional icons. Sanders wasn't really a restaurant in the classic sense. In most eateries, the main course is the emphasis while the dessert is the afterthought. Sanders did offer several light entrées at its lunch counter, but what made it most beloved was its role as a purveyor of sweets—lots of sweets.

Fredrick Sanders Schmidt began his business in Chicago in 1870, but after the devastation of the Great Fire of 1871, he relocated to Detroit. In 1875, Sanders (he decided to go by his middle name to avoid confusion with his father, who was an established baker) opened his first sweet and candy shop at Woodward and Gratiot Avenues. His products were a hit with the public, and eventually, he expanded his store and dubbed it the "Pavilion of Sweets," adding ice cream and soda drinks to his offerings.

In the years immediately following World War II, Sanders stores opened in strip centers and shopping malls throughout the Detroit area. Decades of success followed, making the Sanders stores as ubiquitous as car dealerships and outlets of Cunningham Drugs. At its peak in 1962, the company had over one hundred locations and did some $20 million a year in business. Generations of children and adults would top off a day of shopping with a Sanders ice cream sundae or cream puff.

Local legend purports that the ice cream soda owes its existence to that first Sanders location. Today, the company's website recounts the story as follows:

One evening during the summer of 1876, Sanders ran out of fresh cream for his cream sodas. In an effort to please the store full of eager customers, he used a scoop of ice cream instead. His patrons were thrilled with the taste and word of the new beverage spread. The substitution of ice cream for regular cream became a customary offering at soda fountains and stores throughout the nation.

There are other claimants to the invention of the ice cream soda, but the origin of two other Sanders products is undisputed.

The company's delicious, extra-thick ice cream toppings were sold in ten-ounce jars and came in dark fudge, caramel and a few other flavors. Most people would prepare it by placing the jar in a saucepan half filled with water and then heating it on the stove. When the water began to boil, it meant the topping was loose enough to pour over their choice of ice cream, usually a Sanders variety like butter pecan or Dutch chocolate.

And who could forget the mouthwatering bumpy cakes? Bumpy cakes were made of either yellow or chocolate batter and covered with white buttercream applied in a scalloped, or bumpy, pattern and finally topped with a thin layer of chocolate or caramel frosting.

As a company, Sanders believed in community outreach, publishing periodic editions of the *Sanders Hostess Book* and a daily newsletter, the *Sanders Menu*. Both publications would play off the object of the company's business by centering on a "sweet" theme—extolling kind actions and neighborly charity. Such efforts, of course, were also seen as effective marketing tools.

By the 1970s, out-of-town competition began to steal some of Sanders's thunder. Eventually, the strong local loyalty began to fray, and by the late 1980s, the company was forced to declare bankruptcy. The last stores closed, but the toppings and cakes were still offered in area grocery stores.

In 2002, Morley Candy Makers purchased the company's brands and its remaining assets. But due to the fond memories of many Detroiters for the old Sanders stores, the concept was revived and a few new locations were opened. While the new versions do not offer sandwich or deli selections, patrons can sit down at the counter, have a drink of water from a cone-style paper cup placed in a metal holder (another Sanders tradition), order a traditional Sanders sundae and dream about bygone days.

25
Studio Supper Club

While restaurants are always public establishments—that is, anyone with the means to pay for a meal is welcome to come in and be served—it's no secret that certain places are tailored to a particular crowd and that upon entering, an outsider might well be greeted with stares and suspicion.

When being reminded of this, most people will first think of bars and restaurants near industrial sites. But along the riverfront near downtown, Detroit was once home to such a hangout aimed at local stevedores, or longshoremen—the Studio Supper Club at 4152 West Jefferson Avenue. Situated in an area of warehouses and truck yards, the Studio sat perhaps one hundred feet from the breakwater, adjacent to the Detroit Harbor Terminal. Until the mid-1960s, the Studio was a popular place for hardworking souls loading and offloading freighters to relax after a shift. The work was often scheduled for off hours, prompting the restaurant to stay open the maximum number of hours to serve alcohol.

And occasionally, men who served onboard the ships would come in with their wives or girlfriends for a goodbye dinner before departing for weeks or months at sea. The menu was basic and the crowd clearly not of the fussy variety.

The building housing the Studio Supper Club was sold in 1966 to purported mob boss Anthony Giacalone, who operated a stevedoring business nearby. The industry often relied on "day labor," where an

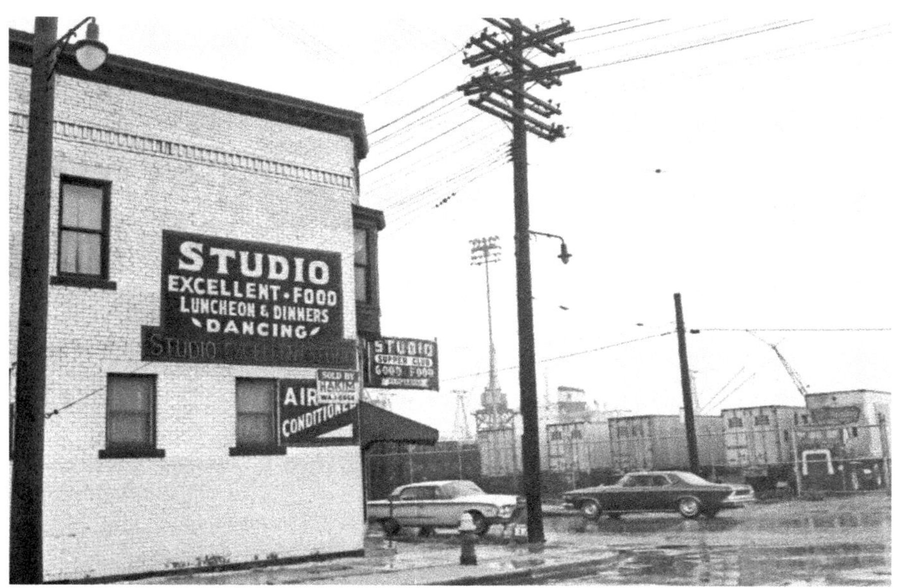

The Studio Supper Club, a frequent hangout for the longshoremen tending to Detroit's docks. *Courtesy of the Walter Reuther Library.*

unemployed person could work day to day on as-needed basis. Giacalone needed space for a hiring office, which he set up on the building's second floor. The restaurant continued to operate for a short time before closing.

26

Tasty Bar BQ

Detroit during the 1960s was a city in transition. Today, many people will recall the changes as simply a persistent downward spiral, one resulting in ever-increasing segregation. And dining establishments were thought to be especially vulnerable. Blacks and whites were generally not given to eating together. During this time, Tasty Bar BQ stood out as a noteworthy exception.

Located at Woodward and Milwaukee Avenues in the heart of the New Center, Tasty Bar BQ opened during World War II, when barbecuing as a method of cooking ribs and chicken became more popular in the Midwest due to increased migration of both blacks and whites from the South.

Tasty Bar BQ was for years known as a small neighborhood place patronized by neighborhood residents. The owners used the traditional southern method of barbecuing, which utilized a vertical-style machine with the coals positioned on the side while the meat rotated nearby on a series of parallel spits. The food would spend a longer period of time in the enclosed vessel, allowing it to cook by convection, or through indirect heat. The machines were built with glass enclosures that were positioned in the front window, allowing passersby on Woodward a tempting glimpse.

Once the time-consuming cooking process was complete, the meat was served on steamed sesame seed buns with fries and sweet vinegar cole slaw on the side. Over time, the place grew popular with curiosity seekers from outside the neighborhood and with the Detroit police.

Tasty Bar BQ eventually closed, and for many years the storefront was an outlet of a fried chicken chain. At this writing, a new chain restaurant is preparing to move in. But it's certainly comforting to know that despite the racial discord of the mid-twentieth century, a place like Tasty Bar BQ succeeded in attracting a racially diverse customer base and contributed, even in a small way, to the city's healing.

Part IV

Saloons, Speakeasies and Watering Holes

For well over a century (save for the Prohibition years), that ubiquitous place called a bar has remained a fixture in virtually all Detroit—and suburban—neighborhoods. Although they do vary somewhat in terms of style and atmosphere, their function has remained constant—a place of respite where a group of friends or a lone individual might temporarily escape everyday concerns while enjoying a pint of beer or a cocktail. There's usually a few extra diversions: a kitchen offering burgers and sandwiches, a few pool tables and the occasional tacky sign bearing a slogan like "my cat can lick your cat" or "one tequila, two tequila, three tequila, floor!"

It wasn't always that way. At one time, saloons (their pre-Prohibition identifier) stood for something surprisingly different. In a 2001 article in the *Detroit Free Press*, Bill McGraw shed some interesting light:

> *Even before Detroit became a shot and a beer factory town in the late 1800s, saloons and breweries were vital aspects of life in ways that are hard to imagine today. Saloons served as a combination library, hotel, restaurant, rec rooms and meeting hall throughout much of the 19th century. The city's first election took place in a bar. One of Michigan's early seats of government was in another drinking establishment, Richard Smythe's Tavern, starting in 1805.*

As public facilities became more purpose specific beginning in the twentieth century, bars gradually took on an identity similar to what we see today.

The rebirth of the legal drinking establishment after Prohibition's demise produced a more relaxed environment. And for the first time, unaccompanied women were able to freely drink in a local bar.

Today, bars and taverns tend to be very egalitarian. A newcomer can often wander in, order and, after being served, strike up a conversation with the bartender or another stranger and may even be asked to join in a game of darts or air hockey. If a television is nearby, it will no doubt be tuned to that day's baseball, football or hockey competition, and no matter how empty the place might at first seem, there's always at least two people nursing drinks while watching and offering loud comments about the latest play.

Restaurants generally want patrons to eat and promptly leave, allowing them to turn the table over as quickly as possible. Bars, on the other hand, prefer that customers linger, confident they'll keep their tab running. At one time, when excessive alcohol consumption was less frowned on, patrons sometimes left in a drunken state, occasionally getting behind the wheel. Today, responsible drinking is the watchword. Movies and TV shows often depict a conversation between a patron and a bartender to be deep and personal, almost like a therapy session, a scenario quite possibly replicated in the real world.

But many taproom conversations have unleashed major creativity. The conception of amazing new inventions or the hatching of promising business deals have often taken place over a beer or a gin and tonic. How often have you heard about an ingenious idea first being sketched out on a bar napkin? Maybe there's something in the booze that stimulates creative thoughts.

While new bars—usually sports themed—pop up almost constantly, Detroit remains home to several very aged watering holes, some dating back to the nineteenth century and still operating today. Curiously, however, many of these establishments have survived despite maintaining their relative obscurity. Most will offer intriguing stories about how they navigated the Prohibition years, which typically involved serving food or "temperance beverages" and/or opening a clandestine speakeasy or blind pig. So while these places are not truly "lost" in that they still operate, many Detroiters may be unaware of their existence.

Scenes of good cheer, intriguing conversation and the occasional brawl were never just the staple of the movies. Scenarios like these played out countless times in Detroit's watering holes, just as they do today. Let's bring a few out into the daylight.

27

The Backstage

Detroit's LGBT community, like that in most cities, has traditionally located its unique restaurants and clubs in clearly defined areas. One of these is on the city's north side, straddling Woodward Avenue across from Palmer Park. Peter Mel opened the Backstage as a small deli at Woodward Avenue and Seven Mile Road in 1978 and two years later moved the business to 17630 Woodward, in the same building that once house the Paradiso Café. Here the Backstage expanded into a full-service restaurant and bar known as Footlights, as well as a small dinner theater called the Manhattan Room, which presented semiprofessional productions of popular plays and shows. The theater hosted a variety of musical and nonmusical productions, aimed at both gay and general audiences. Examples included *Company*, *God's Favorite*, *The Torch Song Trilogy* and *The Perfect Relationship*. This unique synergy made the Backstage a favored destination for both gay and straight audiences alike.

The Backstage made a special effort to emphasize its Broadway theme. Scads of posters promoting various plays and musicals decorated the interior, and even some of the entrées were named after famous stage actors. Popular items included the signature Backstage Burger and the croissant sandwiches. There was also a full dinner menu, including steaks, seafood and pastas. In 1991, Peter Mel sold the Backstage and opened Peter's Place, a much smaller restaurant in Ferndale.

But in 1993, the Backstage met a fate all too common among restaurants. On the blog Detroit Gay History, the contributor, who identifies himself only as Chris H., writes:

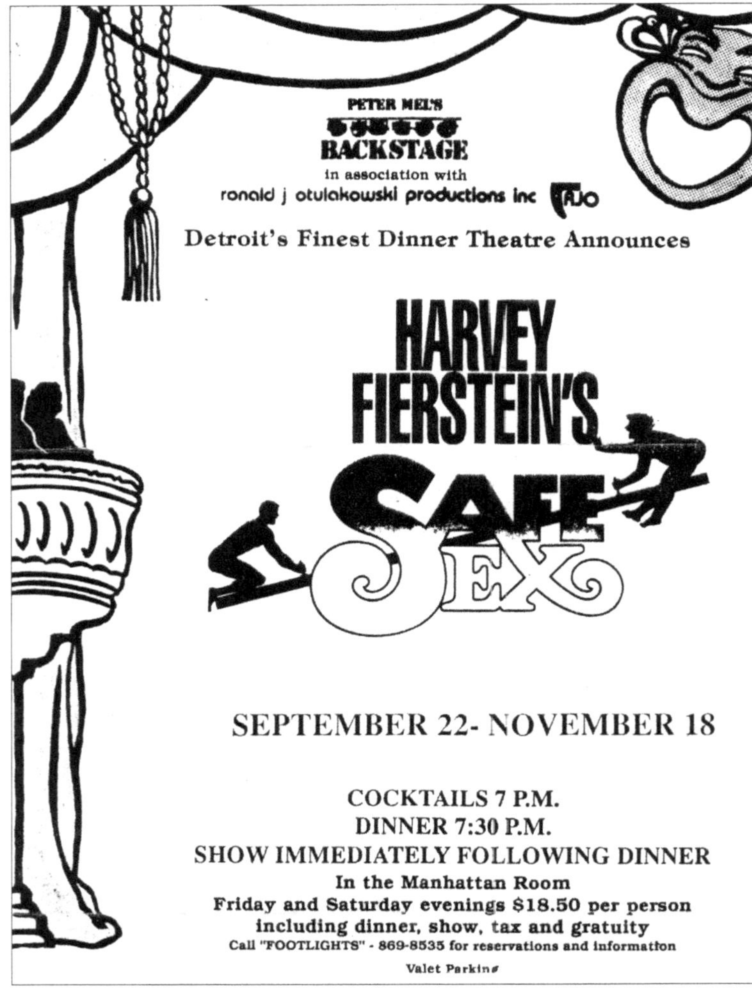

In addition to a popular restaurant and bar, the Backstage also included the Manhattan Room, which offered semiprofessional productions, many targeted to the LGBT community. *Courtesy of Richard Bulleri.*

One night I was at Backstage having dinner with some friends and I noticed this "yellow glow" on a house across the street. I asked our waiter "Is this place on fire?" He said no, it was just the security van which used to drive around with a yellow flashing light on the roof. Ten minutes later he came and said "Everyone out! this place is on fire!" We ran outside and the place promptly burned to the ground in like 20 minutes! I miss that place, everyone does.

Later, it was discovered that a pork chop left unattended in the kitchen had caught fire and was the source of the blaze. The expected high cost of rebuilding the Backstage proved too burdensome. A new, smaller location in downtown Royal Oak was opened a year later but was short-lived.

The loss of the Backstage didn't wipe out the neighborhood's character. Today, several bars and bistros, many aimed at the gay community are scattered throughout the surrounding blocks. But sadly, the exact spot on Woodward Avenue that was home to the Backstage never recovered. In what became perhaps the ultimate humiliation, the site of the original Backstage is now occupied by a mundane laundromat.

28

Cliff Bell's

What's in a name? At Cliff Bell's, plenty! In fact, the heritage behind the club extends even prior to its very establishment.

Arriving in Detroit as a teenager around 1900, Cliff Bell soon set to work for his father, a saloon owner. Experienced in the trade by the time Prohibition began, his sudden unemployment left him angry and resentful. But Cliff decided to do what a *great* many of his peers did—go underground. Opening his Grand Circus Chop House in 1922, Cliff took advantage of his location behind the Detroit Athletic Club, finding an eager clientele among its members. The club, which observed the law and remained dry, didn't appreciate its rogue members' patronage. Eventually, the leadership wised up and made certain Bell's place was shut down.

Next he opened Erskine Bridge Club at the corner of John R. and Erskine Streets, a place without a deck of cards in sight that managed to survive until Prohibition's repeal. After nullification, Cliff returned to operate a legitimate club, opening his Commodore Club, a show bar at 72 Peterboro Street, between Cass and Woodward Avenues. But in 1935, the entrepreneur unveiled his *magnum opus*: Cliff Bell's at 2030 Park Avenue. The new place was Art Deco at its finest, featuring mahogany booths with subdued leather cushions, a recessed stage with risers for jazz bands and a large oval-shaped dance floor sporting a herringbone inlaid wooden floor. A complete bar complemented a kitchen capable of turning out any number of exotic creations: veal sweetbread sauté, boiled smoked ox tongue and broiled Lake Superior whitefish. Dim

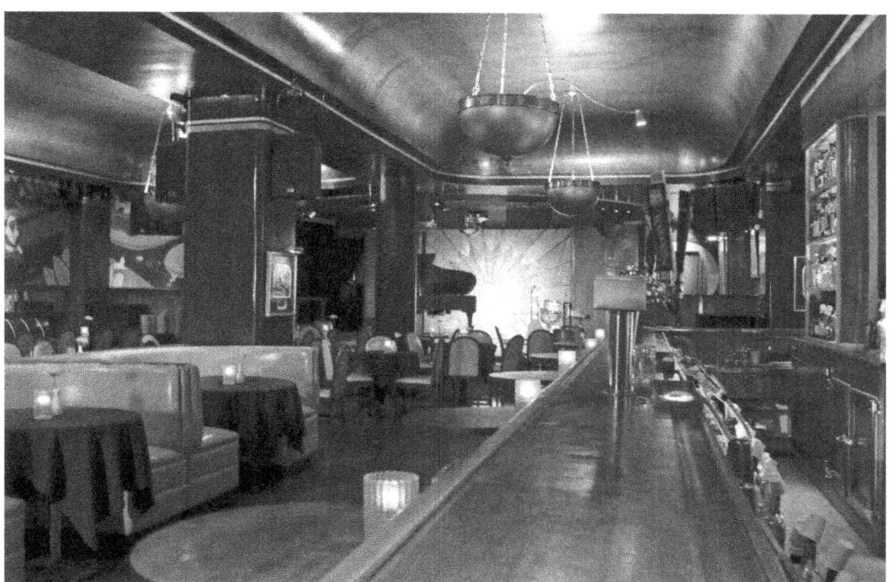

Above: The painstaking restoration of Cliff Bell's is appreciated by anyone who walks in—right down to the polished bar surface. *Courtesy of the author, with thanks to Paul Howard.*

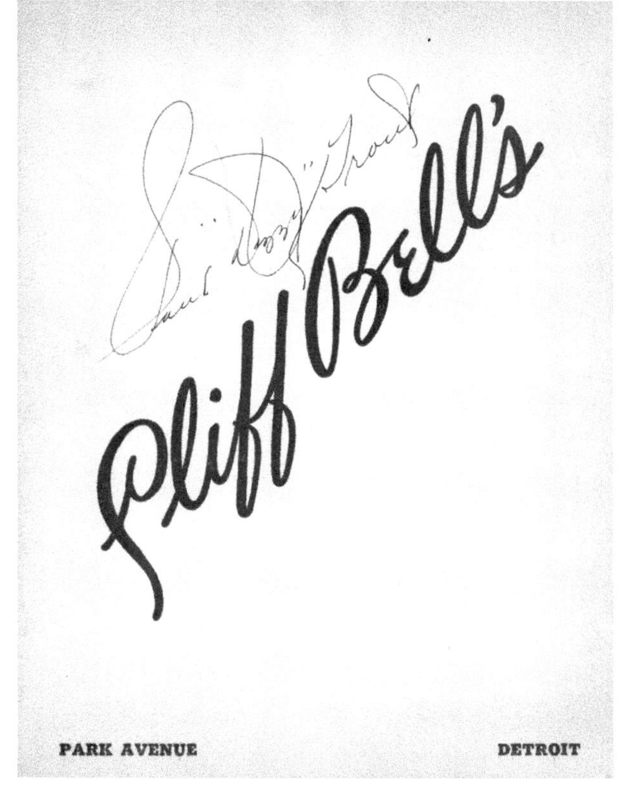

Right: In its heyday, Cliff Bell's was one of Detroit's premier nightclubs, frequented by local athletes and celebrities. This cover of a 1950 menu features the stylized autograph of Detroit Tigers pitcher Paul "Dizzy" Trout. *Courtesy of Paul Howard.*

TODAY'S DINNER SPECIALS

Soup

Grilled Canadian Lake Sturgeon Steak, Lemon Butter $3.15

Choice of Potatoes

Salad Rolls and Butter

★ ★ ★

Soup

Baked Red Chinook Salmon, Fresh Lobster Sauce $2.45

Choice of Potatoes

Salad Roll and Butter

EXTRA SPECIAL

Soup

Beef Tenderloin and Fresh Mushrooms en Brochet $2.95

Small pieces of Choice Beef Tenderloin and Fresh Mushrooms on a wooden skewer, broiled and served on toast

Choice of Potatoes

Salad Rolls and Butter

Soup

Baked Special Meat Loaf, Fresh Mushroom Sauce $1.95

Choice of Potatoes

Salad Rolls and Butter

On above specials no substitutes

★ ★ ★

Our Grill Room will accommodate Private Parties up to Sixty

We Are Open Sundays Beginning September 10th.

★ ★ ★

All Rolls, Pies and Pastry Baked Fresh from Our Own Bake Shop on Premises.

We Age All Our Meats In Scientific, Up To Date Refrigerators on the Premises.

★ ★ ★

THURSDAY, SEPTEMBER 7, 1950

(OUTSIDE CATERING SOLICITED)

Left: Two things are evident from the menu's interior: the imaginative selections and, of course, the phenomenally low prices. *Courtesy of Paul Howard.*

Below: A vintage sign announces Cliff Bell's Happy Hour. *Courtesy of the author, with thanks to Paul Howard.*

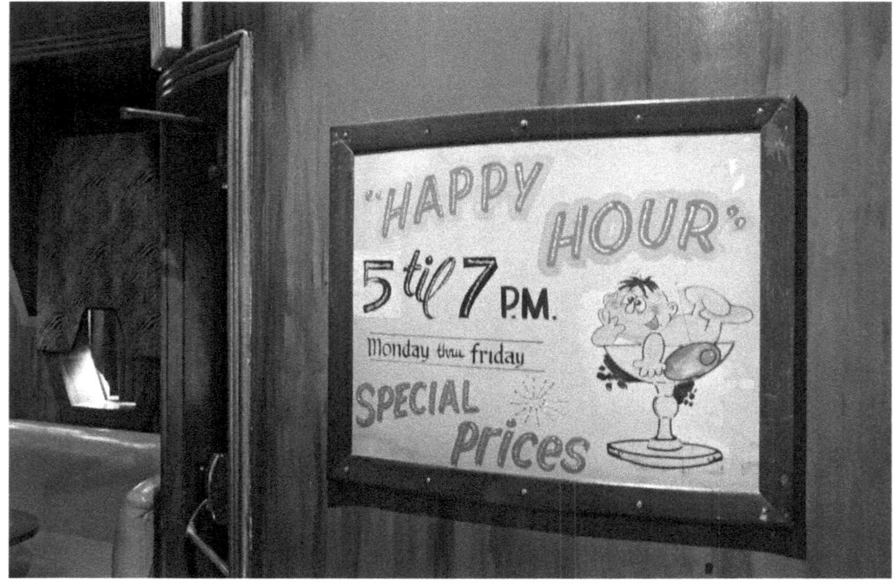

lighting completed the scene. A duplicate bar in the basement handled the overflow on especially busy nights.

It was almost as if the Cliff Bell's was a reward to the city for enduring a decade and a half of Prohibition. Judging from the newspaper coverage of the day, this can hardly be considered an overstatement. A period supplement section to the *Detroit Free Press* included an extensive photo story on the opening of the club and is accompanied by at least a dozen congratulatory ads from food and liquor purveyors, bar equipment suppliers and institutional linen services.

Cliff ran his club for over twenty years, frequently attracting big-name jazz artists as performers and local athletes and celebrities as guests. In 1958, he finally sold the venue and retired. The new owners maintained the format for a time, but the tumultuous 1960s took their toll, resulting in a string of lesser-quality establishments occupying the building until 1985, when it was closed.

But as with many sites in downtown Detroit, Cliff Bell's would be revived to live another day. In 2004, restaurateur and businessman Paul Howard toured the long-closed club at the request of a friend who owned the building. His first reaction to the space, which was laden with cobwebs, dust and water damage, was negative. But after his friend did some basic cleanup and restored the electrical service, Paul was persuaded to take another look, which ultimately changed his mind.

Embarking on a crash course of cleaning, repairing and repainting, the new owners were able to open the club shortly before Super Bowl XL in 2006. "Because the game was drawing close, the city allowed us to open before we had all the required permits in hand, something they wouldn't ordinarily have done," explains Paul.

The subsequent years have been a tough haul, but ultimately a successful one. Today, Cliff Bell's looks much the same as it did in its heyday, offering top-notch music, superb dining and an assortment of libations six nights a week. Paul explains that traffic was slow at first but is now delightfully busy most nights. "Today Detroit is so on the map, people first decide to go to the city and then figure out where to go. Now there's action every night."

29

Jacoby's Since 1904

It's not often that a bar includes the date of its founding in its title. Jacoby's Since 1904, however, is far from typical. What's even more amazing is that the venerable brick building has a history that extends *before* 1904. Built around 1850, the structure at 624 Brush Street first served as a blacksmith shop. In 1890, it was converted to an Irish watering hole called Jake's Tavern, which it remained until Albert and Minna Jacoby purchased the bar in 1904.

Turn-of-the-century Detroit was a city set to take off as the nascent auto industry was beginning to take root. A burgeoning population (much of which was male and single) created a need for reasonably priced places to both eat and imbibe. The Jacobys profited from this largesse, but soon after, the establishment was discovered by the legal and political leaders of the era. Feeling ever more at home, members of the local bar (the other kind) set up a small law library on the second floor, transforming it into a communal satellite office. Caricatures lampooning the profession adorned the walls, and the kitchen churned out Minna's German specialties—steamed knackwurst and sauerkraut, hassenpfeffer and lentil soup, accompanied, of course, by a plethora of lagers, stouts and porters.

Throughout their ownership, the Jacoby family maintained a resiliency and a loyalty to the community not shared by all bar owners. In the late 1980s the bar suffered a fire that heavily damaged the first floor. The customer base downtown was much weaker than today, but the family nonetheless made the courageous decision to rebuild. The floor and walls were replaced by authentic-looking duplicates, and an exact replica of the

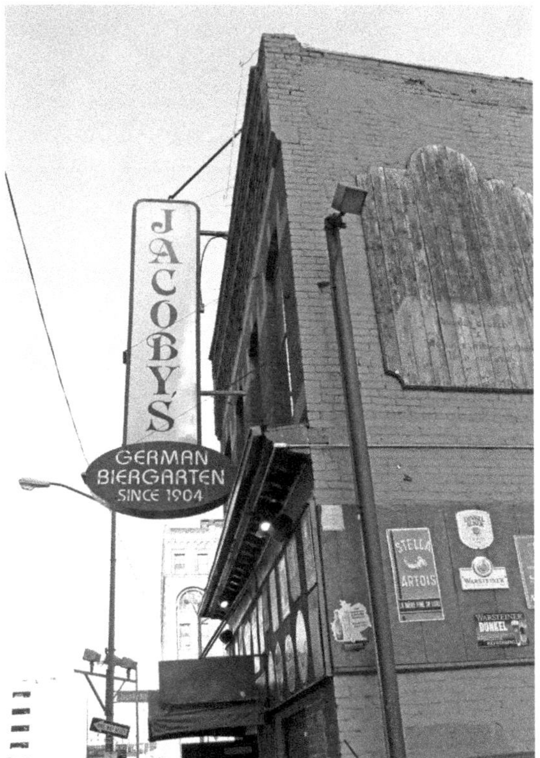

Right: An immovable fixture in downtown Detroit, Jacoby's Since 1904 has served up libations to generations of Detroiters for over a century. *Courtesy of the author, with thanks to Jacoby's Since 1904.*

Below: Traditionally a hangout for Detroit's legal community, Jacoby's today caters to office workers and out-of-towners. *Courtesy of the author, with thanks to Jacoby's Since 1904.*

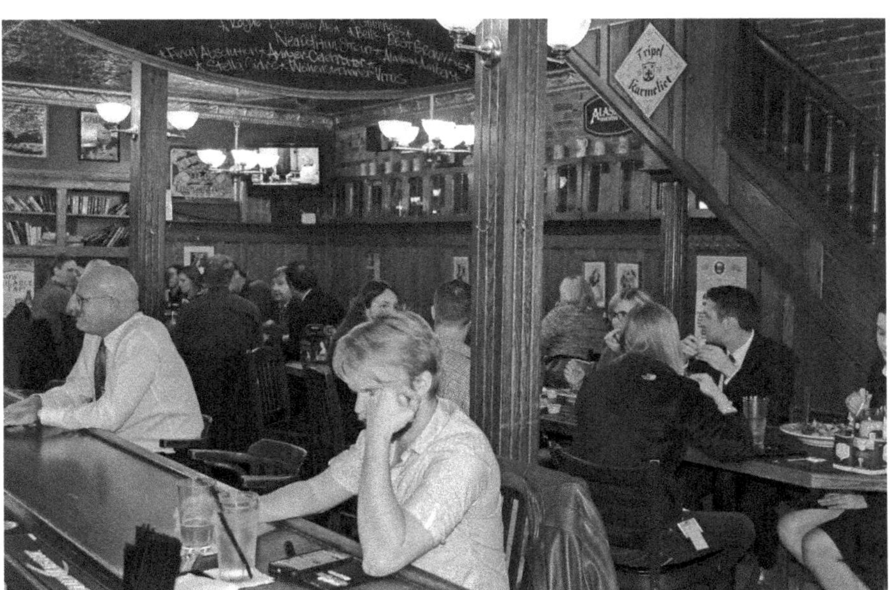

tin-pressed ceiling (executed by the very same Missouri company that made the original) was also installed. The bar itself was rebuilt and moved to the other side of the floor. The work was done so meticulously that a first-time visitor would never imagine a fire had ever taken place.

Jacoby's Since 1904 remained a three-generation family mainstay until 1995, when Edmund, Albert's grandson, sold the bar out of the family. Today, the founding family may be gone, but an array of pleasant reminders survives—an abbreviated version of the law library (now on the first floor), the courtroom cartoons and the heavily German menu. Today's regulars reflect the current generation of downtown types—a diverse group of office workers, lawyers and nostalgia lovers. The upstairs room that once housed the law library is popular for private parties but is occasionally opened to the public on game days.

But the Jacoby's charm can be enjoyed by anyone at just about any time. A visit to the Brush Street tavern with a bowl of French onion soup, a good pint and the camaraderie of the staff is a cozy way to warm up on a cold winter evening.

30

Lindell AC

It's often been said (and not just by locals) that Detroit has the best sports fans of any city in the nation. Not surprisingly, this level of enthusiasm is evident throughout the greater community. Shops peddling sports memorabilia, motorists displaying a Tigers or Red Wings flag from their cars during playoff time and perhaps the most obvious sign—tons of sports bars.

But among die-hards, there's cheap suburban knockoffs and the real thing. Among these, the Lindell AC ranked supreme. In fact, it practically invented the concept.

Meleti Butsicaris, an immigrant from Greece, opened the bar in 1949 with his sons Johnny and Jimmy. Named after the hotel it was located in, the Lindell at first was simply an ordinary old tavern at Cass Avenue and Bagley Street. It was the typical urban bar, offering fare like burgers, onion rings and French fries along with dozens of varieties of beer.

But according to Detroit sports writer Bill Dow, in 1963 the Butsicaris family took a suggestion from Yankee infielder (and future Tigers manager) Billy Martin and began decorating the bar with vintage photographs, old bats, footballs, hockey sticks—you name it. The newly minted sports theme resonated with the public and pro athletes alike and became the template for the concept that is so popular today. And since the Lindell was located near the hotels where visiting teams often stayed, the place became their unofficial local watering hole.

What was special about the Lindell AC was the direct exposure to the players it offered. The tenor of the times did not include the social gap

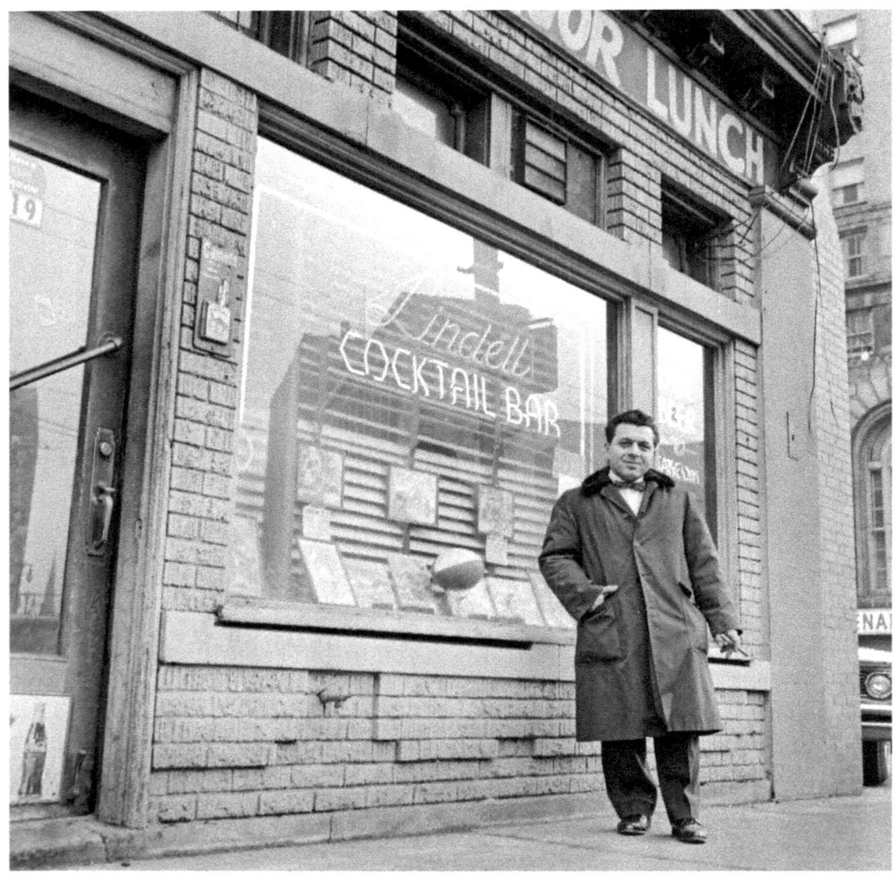

Jimmy Butsicaris, longtime owner of what might have been Detroit's rowdiest sports bar ever, standing in front of the Lindell's original location. *Courtesy of the Walter Reuther Library.*

between athletes and their fans, as is common today. Back then, it was not unusual to sit down for a beer and see Tigers pitcher Denny McLain or Pistons point guard Dave Bing seated at the next stool. The huge salaries of today were inconceivable (players sometimes had to work off-season jobs to earn a living), and team members lacked local celebrity status, seeing themselves no differently than an autoworker or a plumber. *New York Times* sports writer Bill Morris described these times eloquently when he wrote, "It was a time of greater intimacy, rougher edges and, yes, more excess. It was also more colorful, more vivid, in many ways more alive than our high-dollar, heart-smart, smoke-free, sanitized times."

After moving to Cass and Michigan Avenues in 1963, the bar entered its colorful heyday. After securing the 1968 American League Pennant, members of the Tigers headed down to the bar and actually served drinks themselves. Fans recall an incident in 1969 when Martin (then the manager of the Minnesota Twins) got into a drunken brawl in the ally with Dave Boswell, one of his own pitchers—serious enough for both to require stitches. But as the Lindell gradually attracted a diverse crowd, including local politicians and even national celebrities, the rowdiness began to ebb.

After Jimmy Butsicaris died in 1996, John continued to operate the bar until 2002, when he retired. The bar's closing was mourned not just among its regulars but also by it occasional visitors. Dow noted other nearby sports bars—Reddy's Saloon and the Hummer—that closed around the same time, casualties of the Tiger's move from Tiger Stadium to Comerica Park. Today, only Nemo's Bar on Michigan Avenue remains of these old classic watering holes.

Although vivid memories of the Lindell AC continue, there is, sadly, no trace of the building today. Construction of the Rosa Parks Transit Center necessitated the 2006 demolition of the once raucous sports bar.

31

Pinkey's Boulevard Club

Many older restaurants represent a timeless link to a city's past, but when Pinkey's Boulevard Club closed, it ended an especially colorful chapter in Detroit lore. Located inconspicuously in an old house at East Grand Boulevard and Jefferson Avenue (only the name painted in curlicue style above the entrance served as identification), Pinkey's was born as a blind pig during Prohibition. After it went "legit," it became more of a bar/restaurant, but the emphasis was clearly on the libations. A 1978 review in the *Detroit Free Press* uniquely describes Pinkey's station in the community: "Pinkey's Boulevard Club is a near east side clinic for anyone who even vaguely needs cheering up. Pinkey's is one-part whiskey to two parts rowdy good cheer as a remedy for what ails you." The praise kind of sounds like the theme song for the TV show *Cheers*.

Nonetheless, during its post-Prohibition life, the little watering hole did eventually morph into a restaurant—at least partially. Space was at a premium, allowing for only twenty-some tables, including those right near the bar. There was, however, room for a piano. Rare was the time when someone (either a pro or a courageous customer) didn't sit down to tickle the ivories and sing.

The menu contained what we might today call "comfort food" and included steaks, lamb chops, Dover sole and lobster. You might say Pinkey's had it all—food, drinks, hospitality and good times.

But because of its relative obscurity, Pinkey's had pretty much a neighborhood clientele. As the years went by, the old crowd died off, and young people tended to overlook the place. Pinkey's last call came in the late 1990s.

32

The Playboy Club

Post–World War II America was a time of pushing boundaries, sometimes in divergent directions. By the early 1960s, second-wave feminism (the first being the suffragette movement of the early twentieth century) was expanding its influence, as was the "playboy lifestyle" (as championed by publisher Hugh Hefner), which itself grew out of the sexual revolution of the time. The two movements came to tense conflict in February 1960, when Hefner opened his first Playboy Club on East Walton Street in Chicago.

Hefner's Playboy Clubs were stylish nightclub/restaurant hybrids that featured his famous bunnies—attractive young women outfitted in the mandatory costume of a tight satin corset, fishnet hose and three-inch heels, coupled with the trademark bunny ears and cotton tail. Members would pay an annual fee of fifteen dollars for unlimited admission. The first location was an instant hit and became the cornerstone of an empire that spread to over a dozen U.S. cities, including Detroit. Eventually, clubs were opened in several foreign cities with slightly different formats in keeping with local customs. Playboy clubs built around casinos began appearing in the United Kingdom in the mid-1960s following the legalization of gambling in that country.

The Detroit edition of the Playboy Club opened at 1014 East Jefferson Avenue in what had been the Stockholm Restaurant. Like its counterparts in other cities, the club proved immediately popular. On the evening of the black-tie opening gala, club managers were forced to bar entry after

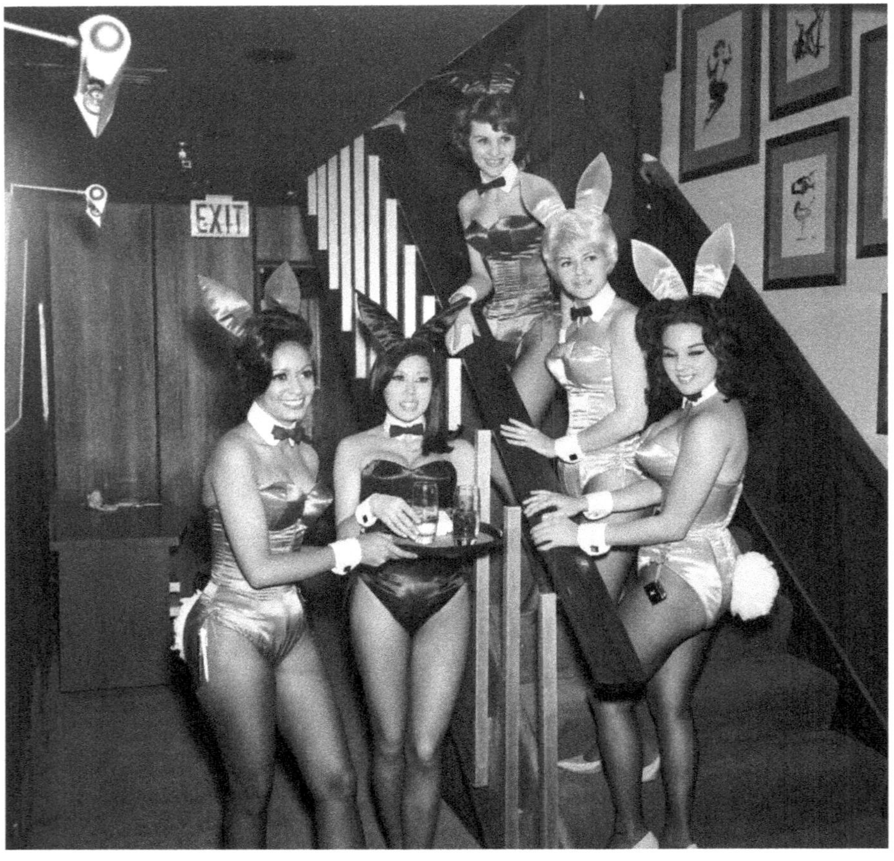

Wearing their trademark costumes, five bunnies work at Detroit's original Playboy Club on East Jefferson Avenue, circa 1963. *Courtesy of the Walter Reuther Library.*

the occupancy level had been reached—forcing newcomers to wait until someone exited.

The Detroit location also opened to instant controversy from various quarters, following a trend occurring at other Playboy Clubs. Unlike other local establishments, bunnies were not paid a base wage and were dependent on gratuities only. This led to picketing by the Waiters and Waitresses Union, which was joined by local religious leaders, with the former complaining about the labor situation and the latter about the bunnies' skimpy attire. On that opening night, some protesters went a bit too far and vandalized the cars of a few partygoers.

Yet another faction was led by local feminists. On opening night, protester Gloria McPherson, wearing an angel costume, paced the sidewalk carrying a placard reading, "I'm no angel but I protest women being called BUNNIES!" while walking her dog.

In 1963, feminist leader Gloria Steinem wrote a groundbreaking article, "A Bunny's Tale" for *Show* magazine (later made into a TV movie of the same name starring Kirstie Alley) that chronicled her experience of working undercover at the New York Playboy Club under the pseudonym Marie Ochs. Steinem explains how bunnies were charged for maintaining their costumes, subjected to unexplained deductions from their tips and told they could date the top-tier "Number One" keyholders but no one else. She left convinced the clubs were sexist and degrading to women.

Bunnies at the Detroit club, however, related different stories. Although they were subject to strict rules that forbade any fraternization with patrons, many found the job exciting, glamorous and lucrative. Often they found their tip income so substantial that a base wage would have been unnecessary. A 2011 article in the *Detroit Free Press* mentioned a few of the restrictions but also the advantages: "The bunnies could earn extra cash by earning merit points for daily good service, or selling the most Playboy mugs to customers. They could earn demerit points—and possible dismissal—for unpolished fingernails, improperly centered bunny ears or an 'unkept tail,' as misspelled in a 1960s-era 'Bunny Manual.'" The mandates of the Bunny Manual were consistently enforced by a staff of female supervisors known as "Bunny Mothers." But despite the strict rules and the patriarchic atmosphere, many former bunnies recall the experience as being a positive one. As one remarked, "We had power. Gloria Steinem was so wrong. We all had lots of fun. We worked real hard—and we smiled and looked good doing it."

And despite the controversy, the clubs retained their popularity throughout the 1960s and beyond. The Jefferson Avenue location closed in 1973 and relocated to the former Boesky's deli on James Couzens Highway near Greenfield Road. In 1976, all the Playboy Clubs switched over to a disco format, a fad that only accelerated their decline. The second Detroit club closed in 1977.

But the nostalgia of the Playboy Clubs never really died. In the fall of 2011, NBC produced a short-lived TV series set in 1961 called simply *The Playboy Club* based on fictitious characters associated with the original Chicago club. The network heavily promoted the series, which led to media interviews with former bunnies recounting their experiences. But when it comes to all things Playboy, controversy is almost a way of life. Attacked by both feminists and conservative religious leaders, the TV show became the target of an advertising boycott. And despite all the hype, the series experienced low ratings, resulting in its cancellation after only two episodes.

33

Tommy's Bar

It's not often that an operating restaurant or tavern is also the site of an active archaeology dig, but Tommy's Bar is highly atypical. Occupying a small patch of land on Third Street, just behind Fort Street Presbyterian Church and less than a quarter mile from the Detroit River, the 1840 building possesses what urban archaeologists love most: multilayered history. Although the building's construction can be accurately determined, little else is known about the bar's earliest history

Over the subsequent decades, the building was expanded and changed hands several times, and it was run in the early years of the twentieth century as s saloon, as well as a cigar factory and barber. Shortly after Prohibition became law in Michigan in 1918, Louis Gianotti operated an Italian restaurant on the first floor.

This is where the building's story becomes especially intriguing. At some point in the late 1920s, Gianotti lost the building to a man named Harry Weitzman as a result of defaulting on a personal loan. By this point, the rumrunning trade—the importation of illegal liquor from Canada—had reached enormous proportions. Profits from bootlegging in Detroit alone exceeded $200 million annually, surpassed only by automobiles in economic impact. Rumors circulated for years regarding the dozens of drop off and distribution points scattered around the city, most in proximity of the riverfront.

In 2012, a joint research project was conducted by the Department of Anthropology at Wayne State University and Preservation Detroit, a community group dedicated to preserving the city's history. Months of

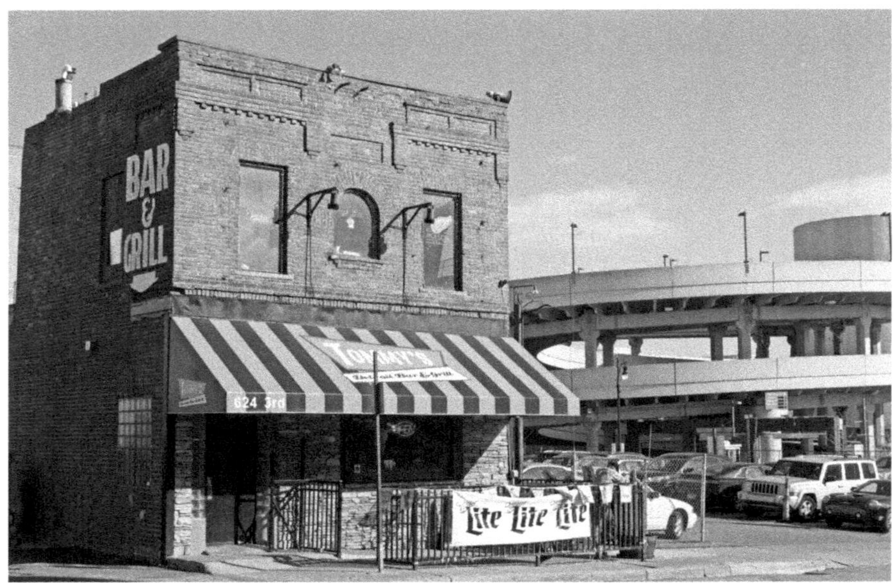

Like a time capsule from the nineteenth century, Tommy Bar on Third Street endures amid the ever-changing city. *Courtesy of the author, with thanks to Tommy Burelle.*

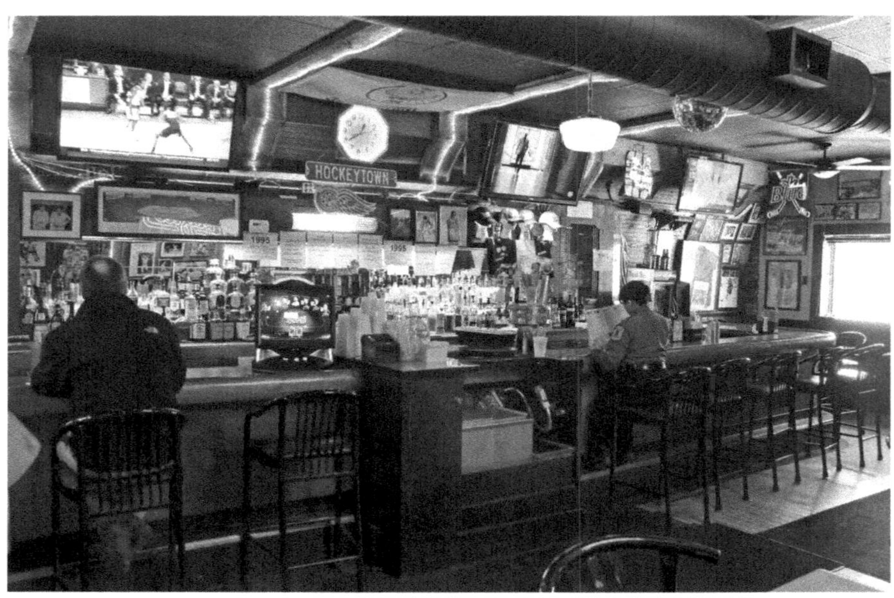

Inside, Tommy's looks like just any other bar, but hidden behind its walls and in its basement, dozens of mysteries lurk. *Courtesy of the author, with thanks to Tommy Burelle.*

research and digging revealed a tunnel entrance on the building's south side that curved toward the façade (its west front) and into the basement. The tunnel does not appear on any city maps of the era and is believed to be an access point to a speakeasy—an illegal drinking establishment frequented by members of the infamous Purple Gang, Detroit's most ruthless organized crime group and leading player in the illicit liquor trade.

A business card discovered by researchers reads simply, "Little Harry." Research indicates that such a card was a surreptitious pass needed to gain admission. The "Harry" referenced on the card is assumed to be the building's owner, Harry Weitzman. Weitzman was a local real estate developer and investor who built the Grande Ballroom on Grand River in 1928. The Grande was known as a popular hangout for the Purple Gang, and Weitzman's association with the ballroom and the bar gives credibility to the theory that the presumed speakeasy at Tommy's Bar was frequented by the Purple Gang.

Curiously, the legendary Little Harry's restaurant on Jefferson Avenue (which also gained notoriety as a mob hangout) was opened in 1935 by a Harry Bianchini. Contemporary research asserts, however, that Weitzman and Bianchini were, in fact, different people.

After Prohibition was repealed in 1933, the venerable bar lived on under a variety of names: Mac's Bar, the Golden Galleon, Thomas's Bar, Tom's Tavern and now Tommy's Bar. During conflicts from World War I through Vietnam, the Fort Street Union Depot across Third Street was a point of departure for thousands of young Detroit men headed for military service. Undoubtedly, many shared a farewell drink at Tommy's.

Current owner Tommy Burelle purchased the establishment in 2011 and proudly caters to a steady stream of hockey fans, convention goers and other downtown types. While Tommy maintains a deep respect for the building's historic nature, he enjoys peeling back its secrets.

And the researchers' next project may be waiting in the wings. The 2012 work done by the team from Wayne State and Preservation Detroit uncovered evidence of a tunnel running from the basement of the bar to Fort Street Presbyterian Church across the alley. The church was known to have several wealthy members during the pre–Civil War era who embraced the abolitionist cause. Speculation is that the tunnel, if it exists, aided in the hiding of escaped slaves and eventually enabled their escape to Canada. Much of this would need to be confirmed, however, through another phase of research.

But another mystery of a totally different nature is also known to inhabit the building. For years, patrons and employees of the bar have reported instances of paranormal activity. Tommy himself relates a few personal experiences:

> *I went into the basement one night to grab a case of beer from a separate storage room. I tried to open the door and although it was unlocked the door would not open—as if someone was pushing it from the other side. I finally threw all my weight at it. The resistance vanished, I fell into the room and experienced a rush of extremely cold air, like I* [had] *just walked into a freezer. Another day I had a similar experience. I went to open the door and felt a strong counter force, which suddenly stopped, causing me to tumble into the room. Immediately I felt like worms or ants were crawling over my entire body. It really freaked me out.*

Tommy relates another story experienced by a contractor doing work on the building. One evening after working several hours, the man took a break and stepped outside. Looking down the alley between the bar and the church, he spotted a mysterious figure—a man dressed in an all-white suit topped with a white fedora and dark sunglasses. The tradesman slowly began to approach the stranger, only to see him vanish a few seconds later.

Stories like these tend to reinforce the convictions of believers, provoke dismissal from skeptics and occasionally alter the preexisting beliefs of those who experience these alleged phenomena. While there will never be universal agreement on the subject, public fascination with stories of the paranormal will no doubt continue.

But this remains just one piece of the legacy of Tommy's Bar. Today, the venerable watering hole on Third Street remains a great place to enjoy any number of beers or mixed beverages, a mean bar burger or some delectable jalapeño poppers in a place filled with almost two centuries of tradition.

Epilogue

Since biblical times, eating for humans has been seen as much more than just an act necessary for sustaining the body. Eating, whether in one's home or in a restaurant, is seen, rather, as a social act, a time when couples or families would share their daily experiences, enjoy one another's company and partake in a shared meal. The choice of companion, food and venue all spoke to one's personal identity. These rituals are universal, in that they transcend cultural or regional identifications.

Since the beginning of the modern era, people have progressively become ever more mobile, increasing the need for places to obtain a meal—and perhaps fulfill the related social customs—at points farther and farther from home. As railroads began to extend into the western United States in the late nineteenth century, the famous Harvey Houses, perhaps the first chain of "eating houses" (as restaurants were then known), soon followed with the purpose of bringing the region a level of decorum previously unknown, principally through their female waitresses known as "Harvey Girls." Here, too, quality establishments that offered both food *and* socialization were seen as a need, not a luxury. The venture proved so successful that it was later mythologized in the 1942 novel *The Harvey Girls* by Samuel Hopkins Adams and in the 1946 movie of the same name starring Judy Garland. You can occasionally see it on one of the cable channels.

During the twentieth century, changes wrought by the automobile spawned different varieties of roadside cafés, motor lodges and fast-food stops—all to satisfy the appetite, rest the body and allow the diner/motorist (should she be traveling alone) to recharge the mind and perhaps linger over a cup of coffee. The era of highway travel might have peaked, but fixtures like these are still a common sight around the nation.

Restaurants in urban areas are held to higher standards. Diners arrive expecting a large array of menu offerings, attentive service and a pleasant atmosphere. And these modern-day eateries also serve as a place for couples, families or friends to engage socially and share their collective experiences, a human need that remains unchanged. Depending on which restaurant they select, they might want Mexican chimichangas, Italian risotto or Polish kielbasa. Over the span of more than a century, Detroit's contributions to the dining industry have met these challenges spectacularly and continue to do so today. This book profiles mainly restaurants that have been consigned to history. While they certainly should be fondly remembered, we should also appreciate the city's vast quantity of newer dining establishments, many of which offer as much character and quality as their storied predecessors. Who ever said a city's dining scene can have only one golden age?

Vintage Recipes

Of all the moving parts that make up functioning restaurant, the food, naturally is the most essential element and represents any eatery's essential character. After all, anyone can visit Easter Market or a gourmet grocer and buy meat, produce and other ingredients. It's what a chef creates with them, how a waiter presents a dish and how the management cares for each patron that truly gives a restaurant its personality.

Printed here are selected recipes from a few of the eateries covered in this book, so you can re-create a bit of that magic in your own kitchen.

Larco's Meat Sauce

2 ounces pancetta, chopped
2 ounces butter
6 ounces small diced onion
3 ounces small diced carrots
3 ounces small diced celery
3 cloves garlic, finely minced
9 ounces tenderloin beef, coarsely ground
9 ounces veal, coarsely ground
2 cups dry red wine
4 cups tomato puree
4 cups seeded and diced plum tomatoes
4 cups chicken stock

salt and freshly ground pepper to taste
¼ cup chopped basil
2 tablespoons chopped parsley

Sauté pancetta and butter in a 4-quart saucepan. Add onions, carrots, celery and garlic and cook over medium heat for 5 minutes. Add ground beef and veal and stew for 10 minutes. Add wine and cook for 5 minutes. Add tomato purée, diced tomatoes and chicken stock. Simmer meat sauce slowly for 1 hour. Add salt and pepper. Remove from heat and stir in basil and parsley. Serve sauce over lasagna, spaghetti or tortellini. (Makes 2 quarts of spaghetti sauce.)

Machus Red Fox Salad Dressing

2 teaspoons salt
2 teaspoons black pepper (freshly ground)
½ cup cider vinegar
⅔ cup Heinz ketchup
⅔ cup chopped onion
⅔ cup sugar

Combine all ingredients in blender and blend at medium speed until onion is pureed. Reduce speed to low and drizzle 1 scant cup canola oil very, very slowly, until emulsified. Store in refrigerator for up to 1 month. (Yields 2½ cups of dressing.)

The Red Fox salad itself used mixed greens, crumbled Roquefort cheese, crumbled bacon bits, quartered tomatoes, crumbled hard-cooked eggs and croutons.

Trader Vic's "The Scorpion"

Around 1961, when a Vic's opened in Washington's Statler Hotel, this was considered quite an exotic drink. Serves 12.

1½ bottles Puerto Rican rum
2 ounces gin
2 ounces brandy
16 ounces lemon juice
8 ounces orange juice
8 ounces orgeat (almond flavoring)
2 sprigs mint
½ bottle white wine

Mix together all ingredients thoroughly, pour over cracked ice and let stand 2 hours, adding more ice. Serve in brandy snifter or bowl with gardenias floating in it. Give your guests extra-long straws.

Hudson's Maurice Salad

1 pound each cooked ham, turkey breast and Swiss cheese, all cut into thin, julienned strips
½ cup minced sweet pickles.
1 head iceberg lettuce
8 pimento-stuffed green olives
2 hard-boiled eggs

Toss ingredients lightly, add the dressing and fold together. Shred lettuce and arrange a bed of shredded lettuce on 4 salad plates. Top the meat and cheese mixture onto each bed of lettuce and garnish each salad with 2 pimento-stuffed green olives and a couple hard-cooked egg slices. Serve at once!

The Whitney's Salmon Gravlax

1 pound salmon filet
½ cup sugar
¼ cup salt
1 bunch fresh dill, chopped
2 lemons

Pull bones from the salmon using needle-nose pliers (or ask your fish purveyor to do it for you). Mix the sugar, salt and chopped dill together. Squeeze lemon juice over the salmon. Spread salt-sugar-dill mixture evenly over the filet. Wrap the coated filet tightly in aluminum foil. Place a weight or heavy object on the salmon filet to press the salt-sugar-dill mixture into the salmon. Let set for 24 hours while refrigerated. Slice paper thin and serve.

Lay thin slices of salmon gravlax in fanned out manner on serving plate with a small pile of thinly sliced red onion and capers. Place a small stack of crisp white and dark toast points or miniature bagels on the plate. Serve with grainy mustard and fresh lemon wedges. The gravlax is great served as you would smoked salmon—on bagels, spread with cream cheese—and is also a lot less expensive than smoked salmon.

Various Detroit Restaurants

Zip Sauce

Generations of Detroit diners have developed a love for something called "Zip Sauce." Originally used as a taste-packed accent for steak, Zip Sauce was later discovered to enhance the appeal of chicken, lamb or just about any meat. The light, thin but flavorful sauce has long been the subject of urban legends, most claiming that the recipe is some closely guarded secret.

Nothing could be further from the truth. Although there are a few variants, the formula for making Zip Sauce is freely available. Here it is:

1 teaspoon crushed dried rosemary
¼ teaspoon dry thyme leaf, rubbed between fingers until finely crushed
¼ teaspoon garlic powder
1 teaspoon dry minced parsley
¼ pound butter, melted
1 teaspoon salt
1 tablespoon Dijon mustard
½ teaspoon coarse black pepper
1½ tablespoons Worcestershire sauce
¼ teaspoon ground cumin
⅛ teaspoon cayenne pepper

Combine the first 4 ingredients and stir into the butter that has been melted in a saucepan. Then add everything else and warm gently for a minute or so. Do not overcook it. Refrigerate in a tightly capped container and be sure to use it within a few weeks.

To use: prepare the zip sauce by stirring about ¼ cup into about ¼ cup of the steak drippings. (Makes about ⅔ cup.)

The *Detroit Metro Times*

In 2013, a reader of the *Detroit Metro Times* discovered a packet of several handwritten pages in a dusty attic in Hamtramck and shared them with the editor. The sheets contained recipes of classic entrées from several of Detroit's long-closed eateries. With deep gratitude to managing editor Michael Jackman, a few of these are reprinted below. Included are original comments that date the pages to around 1962.

Schweizer's

(Celebrating 100 yr. birthday this yr.)
German dishes. Close to Detroit River and the heart of the city at 260 Hastings. Open for lunch and dinner on weekdays, dinner only on Saturday (closed Sundays).

Sauerbraten

Cover a lean, 4-pound piece of beef round in the following mixture: 1 cup of vinegar; 3 cups of water; 2 cloves garlic; 2 sliced onions; 1 cut carrot; salt and pepper to taste; 1 bay leaf and a generous tablespoon pickling spices.

Marinate five days in the refrigerator. Remove meat from the marinade, dust with flour and brown in 3 tablespoons corn oil in oven. When meat is brown, add 1½ to 2 cups of the marinade (depending on the pan size), the vegetables, 1 teaspoon sugar, and 1 diced tomato. Braise until meat is tender. Strain the sauce left in the pan, thicken with 4 or 5 ginger snaps and correct seasoning. Meat should be sliced thin, 5 or 6 slices per person, topped with the gravy, garnished with potato pancakes.

Potato Pancakes

Grate or grind—never use blender—4 medium-sized peeled potatoes and 1 small onion into a sieve. Remove as much water as possible. Then transfer to bowl, add 3 eggs, one tablespoon flour, 1 teaspoon baking powder, and ½ teaspoon salt. Gently mix. Fry in ¼-inch hot corn oil. For thick, fluffy pancakes, slide a spoonful of batter gently into the hot oil heaped high. Turn once, when pancakes are a golden brown, remove and blot. Makes 8 pancakes. Serves 4.

Joe Muer's Seafood

Deviled Crab

2 pounds fresh crabmeat
1¼ pounds 3-day-old bread
5 hard-boiled eggs chopped
1 heaping tablespoon salt
1 tablespoon of dry mustard

1 large onion
1 ¼ ounces Worcestershire sauce
1 ¼ ounces vinegar
3 tablespoons mayonnaise

Cut crust from bread, crumble into small bits, and place in mixing bowl. Add the eggs, salt and dry mustard. Mix well, then add onions (which have been chopped and sautéed in butter) and flavorings and mix well. Add crabmeat. Form into patties and bake in 350-degree oven for 15 minutes. Makes from 10 to 12 patties. Serves 6.

The Caucus Club

Brochette of Beef Tenderloin Polynesian

2 pounds of beef tenderloin, sliced
¾ cup soy sauce
¼ cup honey
¼ cup sweet sherry wine
1 teaspoon curry powder
1 teaspoon salt
pinch of cinnamon
pinch of ground clove
1 teaspoon ginger
1 clove garlic, chopped

Marinate sliced beef tenderloin in other ingredients 12–24 hours in advance of cooking. Broil beef on skewer with cubes of fresh pineapple. Serve with rice and mushroom caps. Serves 4.

Topinka's Country House

Old-Fashioned Coconut Cake

BATTER
2¼ cups sifted all-purpose flour
⅓ cup cornstarch
1 teaspoon baking powder
½ cup butter or margarine
2 cups sugar
¾ cup milk
1 tablespoon vanilla extract
6 egg whites

Start oven at 375 degrees. Grease three round 8-inch cake pans, coat with film of flour. Sift flour, cornstarch and baking powder three times. Set aside. Work butter or margarine until soft. Add sugar gradually and continue working until very creamy. Mix milk and vanilla extract, then stir flour mixture and milk alternately into creamed butter and sugar. Be sure to start and end with flour combination. Beat egg whites until they hold a point. Fold into batter. Pour into cake pans. Bake 25 minutes, or until cakes pull away slightly from side of pan. Cool five minutes, then remove from pans.

FROSTING
Mix two eggs whites, ¾ cup sugar, 2½ tablespoons cold water, ½ teaspoon cream of tartar and a pinch of salt on top of double boiler. Beat until well mixed. Cook over rapidly boiling water, beating vigorously seven minutes until frosting holds definite peaks. Remove from heat and cool. Beat 1 cup heavy cream until it holds shape. Fold into cold frosting along with 1 teaspoon vanilla and one cup of grated coconut. Spread frosting between cake layers, on sides and top. Spring with another cup of coconut.

Bibliography

Articles

AAA Motor News. Review of Carl's Chophouse. January 1962.

———. Review of the Little Café. January 1964.

———. Review of Topinka's. May 1963.

———. Review of Topinka's Country House. May 1962.

Abraham, Molly. "It's Comfortable and Cosmopolitan." *Detroit Free Press*, July 1, 1993.

———. "Life Is Good for Schweizer's at a Ripe Old 110." *Detroit News*, November 22, 1972.

———. "New Chung's Offers the Best of the Old One." *Detroit Free Press*, October 22, 1993.

———. "Roll Out the Barrel." *Detroit Free Press*, May 1, 1983.

———. "Sheik Restaurant Has New Look—Extra Dining Room." *Detroit News*, June 26, 1978.

Anonymous Gourmet. "The Paradiso, They'll Tell You It's the Best in Town." *Detroit Free Press*, April 30, 1979.

Benagh, Jim. "Bocce, Buddy's Pizza: Tasty Sport Dish." *Detroit Free Press*, June 1, 1977.

Braun, Lilian. "Our New Restaurant in the Sky." *Detroit Free Press*, April 13, 1963.

Broderick, Patrick. "Romance with a Capital 'R.'" *Detroit Monitor*, October, 9, 1980.

Carlisle, John M. "Memories Flow as Diners Salute Schweizer's 100 Years." *Detroit News*, June 5, 1962.

Cook, Christopher. "Restaurant of the Year 2012: Joe Muer's Seafood." *HOUR Detroit*, March 2012.

———. "Standing the Test of Time." *HOUR Detroit*, January 2007.

Detroit Free Press. "Cliff Bell's New Bar Is Open." Rotogravure Supplement, July 14, 1935.

Findlater, Richard. "The Clam Shop: A Pleasant Metamorphosis." *Detroit Free Press Magazine*, March 9, 1975.

Gifford, Darcy. "Always Room at the Table." *Michigan Restaurateur*, February 2012.

Harry's Little News. Newsletter for patrons of Little Harry's Restaurant. February 1964.

Jackman, Michael. "Old School Detroit Recipes." *Detroit Metro Times*, November 8, 2013.

———. "Still Standing: Stanley Hong's Mannie Café." *Detroit Metro Times*, November 21, 2015.

Kitzman, Betty Lou. "Little Harry's Offers a Taste of History." *Crain's Detroit Business*, August 22, 1988.

Leduc, Harry. "Jacoby's Since 1904." *Detroit News Magazine*, December 15, 1957.

Leonard, Elmore. "Author Muses on the Mysterious Magnetism of Detroit." *Chicago Tribune*, July 27, 1986.

Lindstrom, John. "Splendid Foods Are the Fruit of The Money Tree." *Crain's Detroit Business*, February 16, 1987.

McGraw, Bill. "City Has Long Ties to Alcohol." *Detroit Free Press*, March 19, 2001.

Monaghan, John. "Cass Avenue's Exotic Chin Tiki Is No More." *Detroit Free Press*, March 10, 2009.

Morris, Bill. "Amid Newfound Glory, Echoes of Old Detroit." *New York Times*, October 8, 2012.

Noble, William. "The Mauna Loa: Million-Dollar Gamble, Polynesian Style." *Detroit News Magazine*, August 20, 1967.

Owens, J.D. "All U.S. Knows It." *Detroit Times*, September 29, 1958.

———. "A Bit of Old France Comes to the Pontchartrain Cellars." *Detroit Times*, February 9, 1959.

———. "The Boesky Brother Act." *Detroit Times*, August 15, 1960.

———. "'The Doctor' Prescribes." *Detroit Times*, January 18, 1960.

———. "A Genuine Italian Touch." *Detroit Times*, July 18, 1960.

———. "History Carries On." *Detroit Times*, November 16, 1959.
———. "New Offerings at Lelli's." *Detroit Times*, October 8, 1960.
———. "Roma Has Fine Tradition." *Detroit Times*, April 14, 1958.
———. "Schweizer's Made Friends in Lincoln's First Term." *Detroit Times*, January 12, 1959.
———. "A Spot to Put on the Dog." *Detroit Times*, July 7, 1959.
———. "3-Feature Darby's Thrives." *Detroit Times*, October 27, 1958.
———. "Topinka's Goes Suburban." *Detroit Times*, May 18, 1959.
———. "A Touch of Old Araby." *Detroit Times*, August 18, 1958.
———. "Vanelli's Gets Facelifting." *Detroit Times*, December 7, 1959.
Paladino, Larry. "Buddy's Grows, but Stresses Quality Over Quantity." *Crain's Detroit Business*, July 7, 1986.
Poehlman, V. "Mauna Loa May Branch in U.S.; Detroit Success Surpasses All Expectations." *New Center News*, January 29, 1968.
Reynolds, Rachel. "Popular Pub Passes." *Detroit News*, July 2, 1986.
Schermerhorn, Jane. "'Top of the Flame' Romances Detroit." *Detroit News*, April 18, 1963.
Sharpe, Sherman. "Dinner as Theater, or a One-Chef Show." *New York Times*, April 2, 1997.
Silfven, Sandra. "The Whitney: An 'American Palace' Returns to Life as a Monumental Restaurant." *MICHIGAN: The Magazine of the Detroit News*, December 7, 1986.
Solomon, Linda. "Mexican Village Has Right Air, but Food's Only Fair." *Detroit Free Press*, January 10, 1985.
Steinem, Gloria. "A Bunny's Tale." *Show*, May 1963.
Sterling, Pauline. "Foul Murder Was Done Where Restaurant Sits." *Detroit Free Press*, August, 26, 1963.
Talbert, Bob. "Buddy's Ranks as a Pizza Valhalla." *Detroit Free Press*, October 11, 1974.
Tanasychuk, John. "Celebrate Oktoberfest at Dakota Inn." *Detroit Free Press*, October 3, 1997.
Whithall, Susan. "Caucus Club Honors Barbra." *Detroit News*, April 5, 2002.
Wilkerson, Isabel. "Tradition Not Enough to Sustain Restaurant." *New York Times*, December 28, 1988.
Woerpel, Jack. "Real Estate-Building." *Detroit News*, August 16, 1970.

BLOGS

H., Chris. *Detroit Gay History*. http://detroitgayhistory.blogspot.com.

Mister Arthur. *Tour De Hood*. https://tourdehood.wordpress.com.

Rupersburg, Nicole. "Reopening the London Chop House: Genius or Wishful Thinking?" *Deadline Detroit*. October 31, 2012. http://diningindetroit.blogspot.com/2012/11/deadline-detroit-re-opening-london-chop.html.

Whitaker, Jan. *Restaurant-ing Through History*. https://restaurant-ingthroughhistory.com.

The Wine Raconteur. "Pontchartrain Wine Cellars." February 7, 2014. https://thewineraconteur.wordpress.com/2014/02/07/pontchartrain-wine-cellars.

BOOKS

Abraham, Molly. *Restaurants of Detroit*. Detroit, MI: Detroit Free Press, 1995.

Burton Historical Collection. Detroit Public Library 100th Anniversary Commemorative Book, 2015.

Demassa, Mary. *On My Own: A Memoir*. N.p.: Xlibris, 2010.

Gallagher, John, and Eric Hill, FAIA. *AIA Detroit: The American Institute of Architects Guide to Detroit Architecture*. Detroit, MI: Wayne State University Press, 2003.

Gavrilovich, Peter, and Bill McGraw, eds. *The Detroit Almanac: 300 Years of Life in the Motor City*. Detroit, MI: Detroit Free Press, 2006.

Maraniss, David. *Once in a Great City: A Detroit Story*. New York: Simon & Schuster, 2015.

PERSONAL INTERVIEWS

The following people generously gave up some of their time to sit down for personal interviews. The information they provided was invaluable in the writing of this book. They have this author's sincere appreciation.

Bacigalupo, Connie. Personal interview with the author, February 5, 2016.

Belcoure, Janet Sossi. Personal interview with the author, January 13, 2016.

Brady, Tom. Personal interview with the author, March 8, 2016.

Burelle, Tommy. Personal interview with the author, February 3, 2016.

Howard, Paul. Personal interview with the author, January 21, 2016.
Keros, Grace. Personal interview with the author, October 23, 2015.
Liebler, Patrick. Personal interview with the author, January 14, 2016.
Pikula, Wesley. Personal interview with the author, October 23, 2015.
Shencopp, Lynn, and Scott Shencopp. Personal interview with the author, February 25, 2016.
Shencopp, Marshall. Personal interview with the author, February 25, 2016.
Silverman, Arnold, and Shirley Silverman. Personal interview with the author, April 17, 2016.
Vesper, Justin. Personal interview with the author, October 23, 2015.
Vicari, Joe. Personal interview with the author, February 17, 2016.

Newsletters

at the Whitney, November 1988.
Harry's Little News, February 1964.

Websites

"Barbra Archives: Unofficial Site Since 2003." http://barbra-archives.com.
Dow, Bill. "Remembering Detroit's Original Sports Bar, The Lindell AC." July 27, 2009. Appearing on the site of the Detroit Athletic Company. www.detroiathletic.com.
LaGrou, Lisa. "Zip Sauce Recipe for Steak." January 20, 2015. Appearing on the site of Oakland County Moms. www.oaklandcountymoms.com.

Index

D

E

F

G

H

I

J

K

About the Author

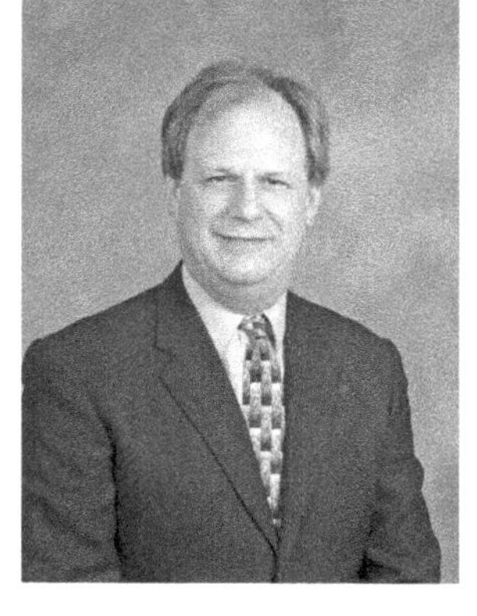

A lifelong Detroiter, Paul Vachon wears several hats—those of an author, independent freelance writer, public speaker and aspiring photographer. After working in the business world for over twenty years, Paul launched his solo writing career in 2008. His favorite topic is Detroit history. This is his fourth book exploring the Motor City's past.

Paul has also written for publications covering a variety of areas, including general-interest magazines, business and trade journals and blogs. Paul enjoys crafting compelling stories through research, interviewing sources and working with clients. Being his own boss is pretty good, too!

Paul and his wife, Sheryl, have been married for thirty years and are the proud parents of their son, Evan. They live in Oak Park, a suburb of Detroit.

You can find out more about Paul by visiting his website, www.paulvachonwrites.com.

Visit us at
www.historypress.net

This title is also available as an e-book

www.ingramcontent.com/pod-product-compliance
Lightning Source LLC
LaVergne TN
LVHW052340100826
845147LV00021B/1131
9781467135597